MAKING MEANING

BY PHILOSOPHY

by
Bob Lichtenbert

Ackowledgments: I deeply acknowledge the constant critiques of this book by Dr. Neil Meccian, my daughter Amy Schialdone, Vicki Elderfeld, Corina Shusheim, Douglas Binkley, Michael Kazanjian, Reid Mackin, Salvador Franco and Dave Lafferty.

Most of these friends contributed responses and suggestions about the many drafts of this book at weekly Seekers' Dialogues held in my beautiful bungalow and blooming back yard (and various restaurants in Chicago) for twenty-eight years.

If you like to be a Seeker, please shoot me an e-mail at seekerofmeaning@yahoo.com. Also, please comment on this book at this address.

I also acknowledge much technical support from my son Steve Lichtenbert.

TABLE OF CONTENTS

PREFACE

This book expresses my views on how philosophy can make much meaning, defined as "positive impact" or effects, for yourself and others.

Much of this book comes from material that I used in teaching the Introduction to Philosophy course for forty years in five states. I nightly revised this material in view of the declining skills of students who increasingly wanted only to play on their cell-phones. Also, they were receiving poorer educations in their schools by far because they were not taught the classic writings of the West as I was.

I much enjoyed such revising because it greatly clarified and expanded my own ideas about making meaning. This has been a big part of how I most enjoyably spent much of my adult life.

I feel highly gratified that the fantastic idea of making meaning that I worked so hard on for many years will now be in print forever for other people to benefit from.

I was inspired to write about making meaning because it clearly struck me as the greatest idea. Further, I discovered that it is the only great idea that has not yet been written about or developed.

I was also inspired to write about making meaning one day by beholding my newborn son shortly after losing a job—I wrongly thought--teaching at a prestigious university. I then realized that **what I most wanted to do with my life would be to make meaning for him and as many others as I could.**

I develop in this book **making meaning. I stress doing it, not just thinking about it. I also emphasize doing so for others.**

This almost doubles the meaning that is made: it benefits the other person and feels good for the doer. What better deal can a person ask for than that? None! (I will answer my questions in this book following them while wildly welcoming yours.)

Making meaning gives you standards to live by in main areas of your life (especially in the chapters on knowing, reality ethics, art, God and politics) rather than just piddly facts. You will thereby get much to believe in. All of us certainly need that.

Everything and everyone has some meaning (impact). No other idea is factually universal, defined as "applies to everything." Again, this is surely our greatest idea.

Please enjoy reading this book.

Also, please make maximum meaning! What more can you do with your life? Nothing! Why else are we here? For no greater reason.

Society would be revolutionized if many people acted to make meaning. They surely would not become what writer Nelson Algren called—with affection!--"nameless, forgotten nobodies."

I will begin this book by exploring the rich, but challenging, meaning of philosophy as pursuing wisdom in Chapters 1 and 2 respectively. Then I will do likewise for making meaning in general in Chapter 3. The rest of the chapters will explain how to make meaning in each field (or branch) of philosophy in this order: knowing, reality, ethics, art, God, the self, politics and free will. I will always indicate by parentheses my references to parts of this book.

"Exercises" after every chapter engage the reader in making meaning herself.

The final feature in this book is that it states main points in **boldface** print to give emphasis and to require less time to read this book if desired.

Again, please enjoy reading this book. I hope that you find it meaningful. That would be highly worthwhile.

– Bob Lichtenbert

Chicago, Illinois
Dec., 2020, "the worst of times,"
(from Charles Dickens in
his <u>Tale of Two Cities)</u>

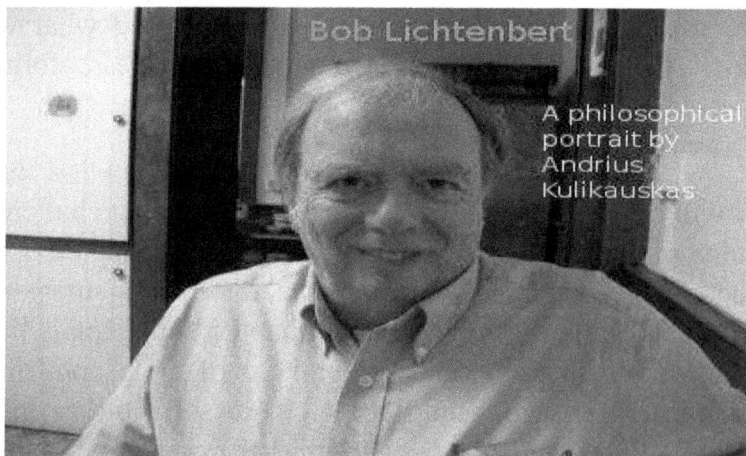

Chapter 1

THE MEANING OF PHILOSOPHY

Philosophy is the highest human knowledge. It can make much meaning for you and but also for others, especially in ethics, art and politics. I will develop making meaning as the totally neglected aspect, actually the essence, of philosophy in Chapter 3 of this book. First let me briefly explain the magnificent nature of philosophy and its greatest goal of wisdom (in Chapter 2) and what they can do for you.

"What is philosophy?" is a huge question so it will be quite hard to answer. Even philosophers themselves conceive of it quite differently. For example, Marxist philosophers regard philosophy as ideas that can make societies just for their workers, but this conception became the corrupt, though very influential, political party known as Communism. For another example, the current dominant philosophy in English-speaking countries is called "analytic" because it analyzes statements. However, analytic philosophers rarely treat life or reality. This explains in part why philosophy currently plays such a small role in our society.

After giving many years to thinking about correctly conceiving philosophy, I now **define "philosophy" as "broadening answers to deep questions about living the most meaningful life."** (Always define any unfamiliar or ambiguous word as soon as it is introduced. See Chapter 4 on "Define Terms.")

In other words, **philosophy develops great ideas to help a person live her fullest, deepest and most meaningful life. A person who philosophizes should arrive at broader and better answers to the biggest questions in her life,** never at a final philosophy. **There are no easy answers to such hard questions, only broader ones that can help explain more reality and make more meaning.**

Everyone has a philosophy or core of basic beliefs guiding all her other beliefs. (See "Philosophy As Your Basic Beliefs" in Chapter 2.) **The main question about a person's philosophy asks how well developed logically, that is, how good or bad, it is.** (See Chapter 4 on the laws of logic.) Most are quite undeveloped and hence infirm. Yet, who wants to be a shallow person with a weak philosophy guiding her life? No one, at least none of my 7,000 students admitted this.

Rodin, "The Thinker"

The typical image of a person philosophizing looks like artist Auguste Rodin's sculpture "The Thinker" where a muscular man strains his every sinew to think hard or ponder. Most commentators interpret that this thinker is contemplating his mortality. (Or perhaps he is trying to remember where he left his clothes as he is nude in his glory! Ha! Ha! He is not "naked" or embarrassingly wearing no clothes, as art historian Kenneth Clark distinguished in his book on that topic.)

THE NINE MAIN FIELDS OF PHILOSOPHY

The most prominent fields or problems of philosophy that reflect the main areas in our lives include the following with the main questions of each mentioned and the field named at the very end of each:

* what are the rules for good thinking, what are mistakes in thinking, what are the main types of thinking such as deduction and induction and what is logic (Chapter 4);

* how can you know big truths (many mentioned immediately below), not just little facts, how can you overcome your skeptical doubts about the big truths of life and what is the philosophy of knowing (Chapter 5);

* what really exists, are intangibles or non-physical ideas such as love and goodness real, what (if anything) exists beyond physical things and what is metaphysics (Chapter 6);

*   what is a truly good life, personal ethics in all areas of our lives, happiness, moral relativism, absolutes, why be ethical, putting "teeth" in ethics, dilemmas and what is ethics (or morality) (Chapter 7);

*   what is art, how can I interpret artworks, art as expressing emotions and ideas, what makes an artwork good, what is beauty as the highest value especially for Plato and what is the philosophy of art (Chapter 8);

*   does God exist or what are the three main logically sound reasons (the   need for a creator of the universe, a divine designer of the Earth or personal experiences of God) for believing that God exists to give me and my loved ones immortal lives in Heaven or eternal fires in Hell— Ouch! That's hooot! Ha! Ha! Why is there so much evil if a good God exists and what is the philosophy of God (Chapter 9);

*   do you have a thinking self (mind) independent of your body or do you have just a brain, what is self-knowledge, do you have an immortal soul, will your body resurrect in a glorified form and what is the philosophy of the self (Chapter 10);

*   what is justice in society, implications of ethics for society, the types of injustices, rights, responsibilities, and what is political philosophy (Chapter 11); and

*   do you have free will (choices) or are all your actions caused by powerful but not obvious forces such as your conditioning, the subconsciousness and genetic inheritance, and how can you choose freely by deeply thinking and loving (Chapter 12)?

In all these chapters, I will emphasize how each field of philosophy can make meaning for you and others.

WHY YOU NEED TO KNOW PHILOSOPHY:
TO LIVE THE BEST LIFE YOU CAN

These nine fields of philosophy are quite broad. They comprise the very foundation for all human knowing and living. Yet, they can be quite complex and abstract. This raises the fundamental question: **why do you need to know philosophy?**

The short answer to this question is so that you can live the best, fullest and deepest life that you can. Do you want this kind of life or do you want it the way it has been for you because it is the only way that you are familiar with? Many people do, but this way might well lead only to unhappiness and mediocrity. **The more philosophy that you know, the better life that you can live.**

Again, philosophical knowing can always be broader, more logical and more rational overall. No one will ever attain full knowledge of any field of philosophy: You can continually know more about each. **As learning this will give you power over your daily life, you will much enjoy it.** (See "Intangibles Have Power" in Chapter 6.) Plus, philosophy is quite enjoyable in itself, as is any study that you can master.

As no human is close to perfect, **all of us can approach excellence by knowing philosophy. The more of it that you know, the more big areas of your life that you can control, for examples, art (interpreting and judging artworks), ethics (doing good acts) and making free choices.**

EXERCISES:

1. Develop as fully as you can one big idea of philosophy such as goodness, justice, love or happiness.

2. Explain why you favor one field of philosophy.

3. Which two fields of philosophy are most meaningful to you?

Chapter 2

THE MEANING OF WISDOM

By studying philosophy, a person can learn the highest knowing of all: wisdom. A wise person combines thinking and acting well. Wisdom begins in wonder about life (discussed in the next section) and culminates when a person gets the ability to use ideas to solve her practical problems instead of fumbling through her life. A wise person knows about broad areas such as ethics, art and politics.

Socrates

Socrates was the first philosopher to address wisdom. He argued that he is wise because he knows that he does not know the full answers to life's big questions. All the other people whom he talks to think that they do. His view of wisdom is negative in that it does not specify what it actually is in a positive sense.

Socrates' main contribution to the pursuit of wisdom is that he emphasized the supreme importance of relentlessly asking the big questions of life such as what is the good life, justice and holiness. Socrates stated that he was on a "mission from God," as do the Blues Brothers in their movie. Seeking wisdom is divine because it is what he thought that the gods do.

PLATO ON WISDOM

Plato

Socrates' great admirer Plato maintained that wisdom involves using reason or thinking to overpower one's non-rational emotions and will. This is the highest human calling. It needs to be embodied in a philosopher-king to wisely govern in order for there to be a just republic (or today we call a "country") where its citizens can best become wise. (See Chapter 7 on "The Parts of an Individual.") Plato stressed that we ought to try hard to fully know Ideas such as beauty and goodness to be wise. "Ideas" is capitalized because it refers in his writings to independently existing immaterial objects, not thoughts existing only in our minds. He has a rather theoretical view of wisdom.

PLATO'S ALLEGORY OF THE CAVE

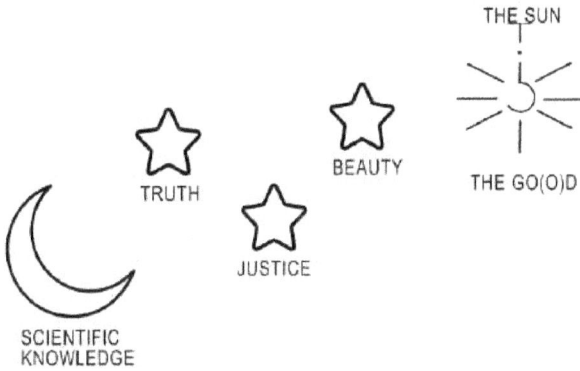

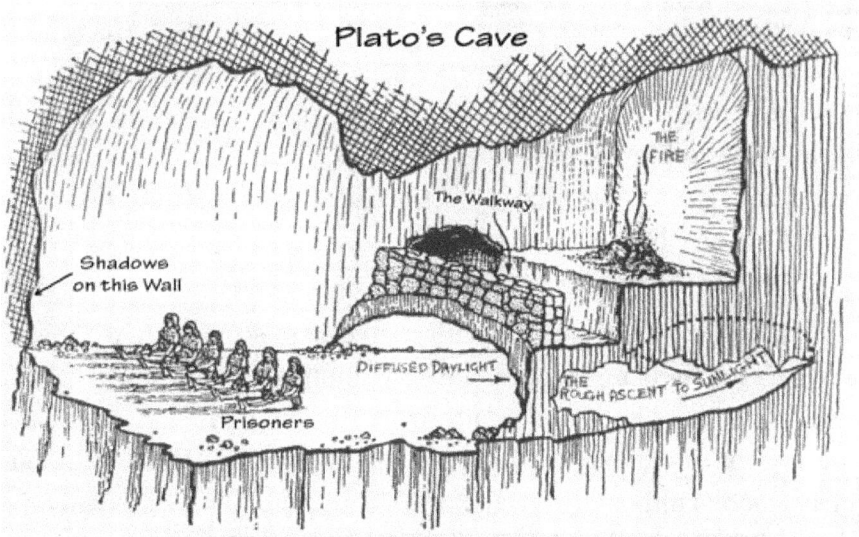

THE SUN

TRUTH

BEAUTY

THE GO(O)D

JUSTICE

SCIENTIFIC
KNOWLEDGE

Plato's Cave

THE FIRE

The Walkway

Shadows
on this Wall

DIFFUSED DAYLIGHT

THE ROUGH ASCENT TO SUNLIGHT

Prisoners

To explain wisdom, Plato wrote a marvelous allegory (or a story with many symbols) of the cave. In it, prisoners are chained by their senses, according to him, to see only reflections on its back wall. (See image above.) The prisoners much need to free themselves from their chains because what they sense weakly reflects reality. They see only images projected by a fire burning behind them, according to Plato's allegory.

I once interpreted this allegory as masses of people mistaking watching television for true reality. **Today, however, I can interpret it as the masses regarding their almost omni-present cell-phones as the true reality.** They are mostly looking at pictures, rarely reading much, even as many of them walk almost obliviously with no clue about or care for Platonic reality. These people are truly prisoners in their cell-phone cave where they see only weak reflections of reality such as stuff to buy. This will all become garbage, much of it in a few years.

These prisoners need to free themselves from their chains to their senses by thinking hard and desiring more reality than weak reflections of it. Then they can scramble up the rough ascent to the greater reality outside the cave. (Again, see the diagram above.) The escaped prisoners should next slowly gaze at the moon which symbolizes scientific knowing, for Plato. Then they ought to look at the stars. These symbolize objective Ideas such as truth, justice and beauty. (See Chapter 6 on "Intangibles.")

Finally, with much difficulty, an escaped prisoner will behold the bright light of the sun. This symbolizes the greatest value of goodness or The Good. This is really Plato's God because he described it as "controlling and causing everything." However, God or The Good is ultimately an unknowable mystery to him, as symbolized by the upside-down question mark in the diagram.

I will mention this insightful allegory of the cave throughout this book. Plato himself stayed high in the sky of intangibles where he excelled, but he thereby largely removed himself from making meaning on Earth. He was rightly quite disappointed by the murder of Socrates, constant warfare and the like. Yet, Plato did have much influence on philosophy and theology in many later centuries.

ARISTOTLE ON WISDOM

Raphael, "The School at Athens"

Aristotle brought his famous teacher's feet closer to the ground, as masterly shown in artist Raphael's painting, "The School at Athens" (immediately above). Under the arch, Plato holds his incomprehensible book on cosmology (or the study of the universe) and points upwards where he thought that all the answers to the big questions reside. On his left, his student Aristotle holding his detailed but influential book— even today! --Ethics, extends his hand downward affirming that these answers are largely found on and for the Earth.

(The other figures in this huge painting are mostly thinkers from the ancient world engaged in various intellectual activities—something that we would never see in our public places today. Also, why cannot current painters produce any work nearly as profound or even as realistic as this one by Raphael?)

Aristotle defined "wisdom" as "knowing why things are certain ways." By emphasizing things, he brought wisdom back down from Plato's clouds to the world in basic areas of our daily lives such as our careers, attitudes, relationships, interests, life-styles, outlooks and the like.

He fully developed not only logic to guide our thinking about wisdom—see Chapter 4--, but also an ethics so that we could have the moral character and virtues to pursue it. (See Chapter 7.)

Unlike Plato, Aristotle systematized political philosophy so that citizens could live together for high common goals, for examples, defense and religious ceremonies. However, he did not delve into making meaning. **The word "meaning" was not even used explicitly yet, nor many centuries later until today.** Philosophy consequently has floundered since then, making very little meaning in the daily lives of people.

The views of Asian philosophers such as Buddha and Confucius on wisdom differ much from western ones, but these thinkers are beyond the scope of this book.

Today's dominant popular view of wisdom in the West and now even the East today is the capitalist one that it consists of acquiring as many possessions as you can for yourself. This is obviously a quite shallow, narrow and selfish view. I will develop making meaning as its alternative throughout this book.

PHILOSOPHY RE-INSTILLS WONDER IN A PERSON

Plato wrote that, **"philosophy begins in wonder." Let's define "wonder" as "the mental state of being curious and fascinated about something." A student of philosophy needs to feel a sense of mysterious wonder touched with a feeling of admiration, even for why we (or anything) exist.** This sense starts her on the quest for wisdom.

Young children often wonder and ask "Why?" However, they tend to lose this when they get older and more practical, including going to schools which now are largely vocational training centers. **Philosophy, on the other hand, much encourages us to wonder our entire lives.**

We now have no end to what we can wonder about, especially the vastness of the universe. We now know mostly by the Hubble Telescope that this consists of trillions of galaxies with each having trillions of stars or suns. (See Chapter 6 on reality.)

We also need to wonder about the tiny small particles that almost miraculously consist of their own solar systems of power revolving at extremely fast speeds. (See Chapter 6 on "How Matter Behaves Mostly Like Intangibles" for many examples.)

Poet John Keats accused revolutionary scientist Isaac Newton of "destroying the beauty of the rainbow" by analyzing it scientifically. However, **such recently-discovered scientific phenomena as Black Holes, time warps, Vibrating String Theory and quantum physics** with its inexplicable multi-verses has now restored a huge sense of wonder to the sciences and the Earth.

Each person ought to wonder the most from her youngest age whether and how her life will have much meaning.

All of us also ought to wonder much about people: why do they do what they do? And how can we help them make their lives more meaningful? There are many other questions to wonder about regarding people.

Finally, **philosophy presents a host of problems to wonder about:** does God exist, will I live after I die, is there more than physical reality, do I have a soul or just a brain, am I free or caused and many similar questions. These questions will be addressed in this book from the point of view of making meaning from each.

Aristotle optimistically remarked that "everyone desires to know."

The sense of wonder is thus very vital, joyful and awe-inspiring.

PHILOSOPHY IS PRESCRIPTIVE
(IT GIVES A PERSON OUGHTS')

In ancient Athens, whenever anyone inquired into knowing something, she was said to be doing "philosophy" This word etymologically refers to "the love of wisdom" in ancient Greek. (This is why the terminal degree given in many academic fields today is still called a "Doctor of Philosophy" [Ph. D.], but all these are fakes unless they are in philosophy itself, as mine is. Ha! Ha!)

Philosophy gave birth to all the fields of study when each found its method of testing, for example, physical experiments for the sciences. Yet, **something distinctive remained in philosophy: being prescriptive. This tells a person what she ought or should think or do** as opposed to what she actually does which is descriptive, that is, summarizes what a person actually does.

Philosophy differs most from all other disciplines because it studies intangibles. (See "Intangibles" in Chapter 6.) **It can give a person her prescriptions because it treats a higher level of reality than descriptions which treats strictly facts or things.**

Being prescriptive distinguishes philosophy as the highest type of knowing. No other type can tell a person what she ought or should do. This makes philosophy quite different from all other studies. **Because it is so different in being prescriptive, it can thereby make more meaning than they can.** I will show this in many places in this book.

This will be an exciting adventure into the different dimension of intangibles! It will also be a journey of discovery on the vast sea of understanding yourself and even the universe! (See Chapter 6 on intangibles.)

ONLY PHILOSOPHY STUDIES DEEP VALUES

Values can be defined as "what a person ought to prefer." Notice how this is prescriptive, not descriptive. Examples of some main deep values include goodness, justice, beauty and big truths. We frequently make value judgments about many things such as people, politicians, actions and even athletes. I can name 418 words that express value judgments. These are sometimes urgent. So, studying values will be valuable. Ha! Ha!

Values transcend (or go beyond) facts into the higher nonphysical level of existence of intangibles. They are more than mere opinions. They capture the objective truth of Ideas that exists external to us, as Plato illustrated in his account of escaping from the cave. (See Chapter 6 on knowing intangibles.)

Only philosophy studies deep values such as goodness, beauty, justice and truth. Almost by definition, these tell us what is meaningful, in the sense of important, in our lives. What more can we ask for than deep values? Only to make meaning which itself is a deep value.

Our society has poor values, for examples, shallow but consumptive materialism and blind faith in God. Because of this, **our values are now in a crisis or a turning point from which they might not recover. There are no experts about values (and philosophy) except a person with her own well-developed views on them**. Why not become such an expert for yourself by developing your values to make meaning with the help of this book?

Every person makes all her decisions on the basis of her highest value whether she realizes this or not. For example, a person will decide even her career based on her highest value, usually either to make money (implies the value of materialism) or to help others (implies the value of goodness in general or altruism).

Lastly, **values are your priorities, especially when goods conflict in a problem.** You solve it by again favoring your highest value. (See "Ethical Dilemmas" in Chapter 7.) So, again, why not know about deep values? That would be among the best thinking that you can do.

PHILOSOPHY IS YOUR BASIC BELIEFS

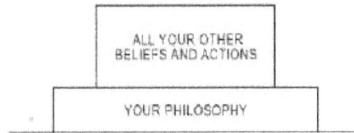

Your philosophy consists of your basic beliefs. This is due to the fact that your philosophy is your fundamental or foundational beliefs about every major area of life (indicated in the following parentheses) such as ethics (your behavior), God (your religious beliefs) and art (your art criticism).

Your basic beliefs determine or guide all your actions. For example, your ethics determine what you will do in a moral situation such as whether or not to lie.

Finally, your basic beliefs make up your assumptions about everything that is important to you, for examples, God and free will.

Again, everyone has a philosophy. You can have either a good or bad one. A good philosophy is well developed and logically thought about. Why not have a good philosophy since it gives wisdom, restores your sense of wonder, teaches deep values and is your basic beliefs that guide your major actions? That would be truly excellent!

EXERCISES:

1. Describe anyone whom you consider wise.

2. What do you think you should wonder about the most? Why?

3. Specify as many prescriptions or ought's/should's as you can.

4. Define your three highest values. (See the Chapter 4 on "Define Terms.")

5. Name two of your basic philosophical beliefs.

Chapter 3

MAKING MEANING IN GENERAL

Now I will explain what is making meaning in general so that I can apply it in following chapters to all the nine main fields of philosophy listed in Chapter 1 to show how you can make meaning in each field. Recall from the "Preface" that everything has some meaning in its relations to or effects on other things.

Following the laws of logic, **I defined (on page 1) the unfamiliar and ambiguous phrase "making meaning" as "having a positive impact." This phrase refers to the beneficial effects that a person has on herself and others as making meaning.**

I will use "making meaning" primarily in this positive sense. I will rarely treat negative meaning which I call "meaninglessness," in the unusual sense of "negative effects." Meaninglessness abounds, for examples, in the countless economic injustices in jobs around the world and in the inexorable death of every living organism. We much need to lessen it in our lives. Again, however, this book will concentrate on the positive aspects of making meaning.

A prominent positive sense of the word "meaning" is someone's "purpose" or "goal" in acting. Having a purpose can much motivate or move a person to act. Many of us very much need a purpose rather than just thinking about it.

"Meaning" is, in effect, synonymous with all positive or affirmative words. I myself have identified seventy positive senses in which I have used "meaning" in the sixty-two issues of my quarterly journal, "The Meaning of Life." (This journal went viral with 3,400 subscribers.) Some examples of these positive senses of "meaning" include "importance," "significance" and "specialness."

According to this definition, **meaning is somewhat objective** or exists outside a person's mind because it refers to the physical impacts or effects that a person (or thing) has. This word is not totally subjective as it is widely assumed today.

"Making meaning" differs much from the "meaning of life." Most briefly, the former phrase concentrates on making positive impacts in many activities in one's daily life, whereas the latter focuses on the broad purpose that every person should aim at in her life.

MOTIVATING MAKING MEANING

John Dewey   *Albert Camus*

Jean-Paul Sartre

I will now try to motivate the reader to make meaning by giving her the following main reasons for doing so.

Making meaning:

ought to matter because of its positive impacts or effects in your life, almost by definition, as just explained;

answers the ultimate question about why do any action—because of the meaning that it will have;

tells us what has value, or as John Dewey, the pragmatist dean of American philosophy, colloquially defined as what a person ought to "prize" or cherish" because it has meaning to her;

ennobles a person to strive mightily against the plentiful absurd meaninglessness in her life to scorn it by asserting her free will to make meaning as existentialist philosophers Albert Camus and Jean- Paul Sartre implied;

makes one virtually righteous in the Biblical sense of following spiritual laws; and

gives a person adult joy rather than childish fun.

What greater motivation can there be than making meaning? Very little!

HOW TO MAKE MEANING FOR ONESELF

A person can make meaning in two main areas: for herself and others. The following five paragraphs briefly summarize the main ways in which a person can make meaning for herself in general.

To make meaning for yourself, you need to benefit yourself in some way such as the educational, recreational, familial, spiritual, financial and the like.

The primary way to make meaning for yourself is to refine your reasoning ability overall to think hard of various ways in which you can make meaning. Reading serious material is the best way to do this, although it requires years. Reading such material is among the hardest tasks for a human to achieve. Our minds are not very gifted at abstract thinking. We can conceive of such huge concepts as infinity and eternity, but we certainly cannot know much about them. **Despite such limitations, reading can do the most to make meaning for individuals by indirectly training and improving a person's ability to think of possible ways to do so (and much more).**

The second main way to make meaning for oneself is to strongly will or desire to do it. This is similar to caring about or having an interest in something. Every person ought to very much want to make meaning. This strong will-to-make-meaning in a person needs to be applied to her ideas generated by the first main way to make meaning for yourself. **Only the person herself can motivate her will much**. Motivating depends much more on the will than reasoning.

The third main way to make meaning for oneself is by cultivating positive feelings at least for their own sake, for examples, love, peace and freedom. These ought to affirm life in general. That alone makes much meaning for a person. All of us should have strongly positive feelings for the need to make meaning. **Strongly felt feelings, especially affirmative ones, make the most meaning to an individual by far** rather than dry ideas. As in the second way, thinking of an idea can hardly motivate one's will or emotions because these are non-rational, as Plato noticed long ago. (See Chapter 7 on his account of the faculties of an individual in "Why Be Ethical.")

The overall goal of making meaning for oneself is to live fully and richly. Get as many enriching experiences as you can, for examples, close human interactions, fulfilling work, ethical actions and interpreting artworks. **You need to find something meaningful that makes you feel happy over everything else.** (See "Sources of Making Meaning" shortly below.)

If you make much meaning for yourself, your life will be like that of banker George Bailey in the classic Christmas movie "It's a Wonderful Life." When he thinks about committing suicide because his life lacks meaning an angel shows him—spoiler alert!--how much he would have been missed if he had not existed.

The main way to make meaning for other people is to pro-actively help them satisfy their needs. You can do this in many concrete and specific ways. The following lists just a very few of them: helping neighbors with their homes, cars and yards; consoling someone who has suffered a loss or death of a loved one; and engaging others in intelligent conversations.

ESCAPING MAKING MEANING

Making meaning for yourself and others requires sacrificing what might well be meaningful to you such as time, energy and money. However, it is often worth the effort to make because it almost doubles meaning (yet still again, for yourself in feeling good about doing it as well as the other person who gets your positive impacts).

Making physical or mental meaning is rarely easy work. **For this reason many people frequently engage in escaping from or avoiding making meaning because of its difficulty. They then keep mindlessly busy distracting themselves. Some of them are even honest enough to admit that they sometimes are just "killing time"** by, for examples, playing on their cell-phones, video gaming, moderate drinking of alcohol and watching worthless movies, spectator sports and TV programs which abound. There are legions of other examples of such escapes . . .

Escaping from making meaning as a life-style results in utterly contemptible mediocrity--unless a person already is mediocre. Ha! Ha! Escapes cowardly avoid living one's own life fully and richly. They "sell out," to use a phrase popular in the 1960's, their precious meaning.

A person can avoid or escape escaping meaning mostly by emphasizing the rich rewards of making meaning, for examples, its feeling of joy (rather than just fun) and its sense of fine personal achievement. We can also much escape such escapes by frequently

engaging in the next topic.

SOURCES OF MAKING MEANING

To escape escapes, much of the meaning that you make for yourself and others comes from what I call "the sources" (or avenues) of making it. Since these are too long to summarize here, I refer the reader to my book <u>Making Meaning</u> (2016) for a full treatment of them, but the following most briefly summarizes these main sources:

maintaining quality relationships of approximately equal giving and taking between two people;

having a sense of community in uniting with other people often known on a first-name basis to work toward common social goals;

working at a fulfilling or rewarding career;

owning needed possessions, not luxuries;

searching for God or the spiritual (See Chapter 9 on arguments for the existence of God.);

knowing intangible truths such as those about goodness or ethics, justice, free will and love (See Chapter 6 on "Intangible Truths"); and

interpreting (or explaining meanings in) artworks, judging them as good or bad and appreciating their beauty. (See Chapter 7 on art.)

I conclude this list by stating that **there are very many other sources of making meaning,** for examples happiness and peace. **Make all these as big in your life as you can.**

MAKING MEANING BY PHILOSOPHY IN GENERAL

I have now summarized making meaning for yourself and other people. How can a person make meaning by philosophy in general?

First, the reader needs to become explicitly aware of her basic beliefs in the nine main fields of philosophy listed in Chapter 1. This alone will give her much fundamental knowledge about all big areas of reality. It will much distinguish her from the masses who do not have a clue about what this is and so they stumble through their lives. On the other hand, the reader of this book will get continually broader, but specific, answers to life's deepest questions such as what is good, just, beautiful and true. **Studying philosophy for making meaning thus gives you an amazingly big, but precise, views on deep thinking and then acting.**

Philosophy is the most advanced type of knowing. It is not needed if all you want to do is survive like an animal, **but making meaning by philosophy is needed if you want to thrive or prosper as a person. Yet still again, all of us ought to want to bloom like a glorious flower** rather than invasive weed.

Advanced knowing makes up philosophy. Its goal is wisdom as discussed in the Chapter 2. This involves applying intangible truths or Reformed Platonic Ideas, particularly goodness and justice which are Ideas about our acting to better understand our daily lives. This is far from easy because ideas are abstract and general whereas the world is quite concrete and specific. **Yet, the two realms do meet or overlap because they are connected. When a person finds a connection of intangible truths to her life, she can make much meaning, indeed. Her experience is enriched. She escapes from the dark cave of her sensing into the bright Platonic realm of Ideas (yet again, capitalized because they exist independent of our minds, for him). Making meaning through philosophy thus can do much to raise the quality of a person's life.**

Only a person's philosophy gives her basic truths. They direct or guide any major decision or action that she makes. For example, a person will do that action which her idea of the ethical good tells her that she ought to do. **Philosophy gives deep advice about acting and living after reflecting much.** This is no small gift!

Only knowing one's philosophical values, almost by definition, tells a person what are her priorities and what ought to matter most to her. What other study than philosophy can bring more logically well-developed broad but specific truths, deep values, wisdom and joy? None comes close! Studying philosophy can make much meaning now that it has been explained here.

To summarize this chapter, we now know what is making meaning in general, motivating oneself by much willing to make it, making it for yourself and others, escaping escapes from it, the many sources of making meaning and making meaning by philosophy in general.

Before applying this knowledge to each field of philosophy, we all need to know how to think correctly about such complex topics. So we will next turn to logic and its laws.

EXERCISES:

1. Explain why you need to study philosophy in general drawing from reasons presented in this chapter or perhaps some of your own. Write your basic belief for every one of the nine fields of philosophy.

2. How did knowing your highest values helped you make a major decision in your life?

3. Explain how one philosophical value helped you to identify one of your priorities.

4. What is the most important source of meaning to you?

Chapter 4

THE UNIVERSAL LAWS

OF LOGIC

All of us obviously need to know how to think well or logically about every topic, especially making meaning. Logic tells us how to do this. It is the field of philosophy that studies the laws of sound thinking. **These laws can tell us which piece of thinking, including opinions, is sound.**

Logic differs much from all the other fields of philosophy. These speculate highly on broad areas of reality such as human nature and the philosophy of knowing. **We will often need the laws of logic to guide our thinking as we study the advanced thinking involved in philosophy and making meaning.** That is the reason that this non-speculative chapter is placed in this book before all the speculative fields of philosophy. **The reader might want to skip this chapter and proceed to these fields now.**

As I stated just above, logic gives us laws in accordance with which all of us should philosophize, think about making meaning and think in general. **The laws of logic ought to govern all our thinking, just as philosophy ought to govern all our lives.**

Logic by its laws provides objective tests whether any piece of thinking is strong or weak. Knowing these more could do much to lessen today's widespread relativism according to which no opinion can be shown to be more sound than any other. This way of thinking can even be dangerous as well as chaotic. (See Chapter 7 for more on relativism.)

Thus, logic gives us much-needed standards to evaluate even all our opinions, value judgments and the like. These make up an extremely large and important part of our thinking. Knowing the facts is just the start of logical thinking.

The laws of logic apply to all people in all societies at all times. These laws are thus universal. We ought to always apply them to all thinking. **These laws can help us think more logically and communicate clearly**. However, because of the complexity of human thinking, a thinker might have difficulty applying the laws of logic to a piece of reasoning.

Aristotle, the father of logic

Aristotle started logic by writing several treatises (short books) on this topic. With these writings he fully developed logic except the mathematical aspects of deduction (see shortly below), which was done around the start of the twentieth century.

The rest of this chapter will concern itself with briefly explaining the basic laws of logic, starting with the ones for thinking in general.

1. THINK IN TERMS OF "ARGUMENTS"

The first law of logical thinking is to organize your thinking into what logicians call an "argument." This is a special sense of this word (which should always be specified according to Section 3 on defining terms below), not its usual sense of a "disagreement." **Instead, an "argument" in logic refers to the smallest unit or a piece of logical thinking to make a point or conclusion. An "argument" is defined as "reason(s) given as premises to support a conclusion."**

In an argument, the reasons given to support a conclusion are called "premises." These are evidence or grounds used to support or back up a conclusion. A logical thinker needs to make sure that the facts in her premises are true according to the laws of induction. (See Section 2.) She also needs to ensure her opinions in her premises follow validly according to the laws of deduction. (Again see Section 2.)

The conclusion of an argument is the point that it tries to make. In other words, the conclusion is the judgment reached by its premises or what they imply. **Again, premises give evidence (or reasons or grounds) for believing that the conclusion is true.**

Diagram of a logical argument:

Premise (evidence or reason that supports the conclusion)
Other premise(s) (more evidence that supports the conclusion)

Conclusion (the point of the argument that needs to follow "soundly," defined as "both inductively true and deductively valid"—explained in Section 2.)

This diagram is too mechanical to be used for the messiness of everyday thinking, but it does show the underlying structure of a logical argument.

2. USE THE TWO TYPES OF LOGICAL ARGUMENTS: INDUCTION AND DEDUCTION

"There is . . . a double movement in all reflection," wrote progressive educator and American philosopher John Dewey. He was referring to the two logical types of thinking called "arguments": induction and deduction.

A. **INDUCTION** is an argument composed of physical observations or experiences or facts. It argues from particular experiences (sometimes called "examples" or "cases") to generalizing about them in the conclusion.

Diagram of an inductive argument:

particular statement (premise)
other particular statement(s) (premise[s])

---

general statement (conclusion)

EXAMPLE of an inductive argument:

This swan is white. (particular premise)
That swan is white. (particular premise)
Those swans are white.

Therefore, all swans are white. (general conclusion)

In a sound induction that follows all its laws—these laws are not summarized here because they are not major--the conclusion follows at best with much probability, not absolute truth. Your experiences can be contradicted the next time. For example, if you travel to Australia, you can see black swans there.

The natural and social sciences use induction because it observes the world and people respectively. Its laws concern how to conduct experiments leading up to the well-developed scientific method—too big to be summarized here--that has been highly productive in its applied form of technology. **All of us ought to use induction to think logically about factual or physical matters.**

B. DEDUCTION in many ways reverses induction, as Dewey noted. **Deductive arguments use generalizations in their premises. Then these infer or "squeeze out" a more specific conclusion.**

Diagram of a deductive argument:

generalization (premise)
generalization (premise)

---

particular statement (conclusion)

EXAMPLE of a deductive argument:

All men are mortal. (premise) (Socrates argued that this is false.)

Socrates is a man. (premise)

Therefore, Socrates is mortal. (conclusion)

Deduction is a purely mental process which does not involve experimenting with the physical world. Since it involves just **thinking about matters sheerly mental or in one's mind, the conclusion of a sound deduction follows with necessity,** not just probability as inductions do. The generalizations in a deduction either correctly relate to each other according to its laws. (These laws are not summarized here.) **A correct deduction is technically called "valid."** The premises of a deduction are assumed to be true, but (again) they should be critically examined for their truth by the laws of inductive thinking before they are accepted as premises.

All the fields of philosophy and mathematics rely on deduction exclusively. **We ought to use it to determine the soundness of all opinions, value-judgments and all other non-factual arguments which are frequent in our thinking, as I have emphasized.**

As deduction is a totally theoretical type of logical thinking, it helps little to improve one's logical thinking abilities. It does help us understand our abstract thinking.

Like induction, deduction gives us objective tests of the soundness of our thinking by giving us laws for it that arguments needs to follow. Surely, such objective tests as induction and deduction help us to think logically about making meaning (and all subjects).

After you know the laws for logical arguments, you can say with detective Sherlock Holmes whenever you solve a problem such as a murder by using them, as he did, "It's elementary!" It truly is if you think in terms of arguments.

3. DEFINE AMBIGUOUS TERMS

Other laws of logic that can much help to improve communicating as well as logical thinking. These laws concern the use of words. This is a highly meaningful area of logic because the symbolic nature of language enables humans to think abstractly which other animals cannot do.

Winston Churchill

The British prime minister Winston Churchill asserted that, "The most important thing that can be gained from an education is a thorough . . . command of one's native language." A master of it himself, he thereby made much meaning, especially in much helping to end the horrors of World War II with his eloquence. **Knowing the laws of the logic of language can make meaning for us too with words that we all use every day just as Churchill did.**

The most important laws regarding logic and language involves defining terms. **The first law of definition is to always define an ambiguous or an unfamiliar term as soon as it is introduced,** for examples, "meaning" defined as "positive impact" on page 1 of this book and "philosophy" defined at the start of Chapter 1.

To "define" a word refers to "specifying exactly what it refers to." Its etymology, is "to set limits or boundaries" on a term. Defining a word always ought to clarify its meaning.

Another main law regarding language and logic is to use words as they are defined in a dictionary which can now be done by Googling them. Again, if you need to use a word in a special sense, be sure to specify the precise sense in which you use it, for example, as done for "argument" earlier in this chapter. Many words have many senses in which we use them. For example, the word "strike" has dozens of them.

To best define a word, the first law is to think of the general class of things that it shares essential traits with. Aristotle called this the "genus" of a word. For example, the genus of "humans" is "animals," not a broader or narrower class such as "minerals."

Then you need to think of the specific respect in which the word differs from everything in its general class. Aristotle called this a word's "specific difference," for example, "rational" for "humans." The logical definition of "humans" is thus that they are "rational animals." This definition still holds despite Freud's emphasis on how irrational humans are. We can similarly define all terms by thinking first of its genus and then its specific difference.

Aristotle thus gave us helpful laws for defining words to think logically and communicate clearly about them. **Defining unfamiliar** and ambiguous words ought to often serve as the starting point to make meaning in all thinking and talking. **It rarely is,** even in long talks and writings about a topic. Ignorance of the laws of logic fails to make meaning, even linguistically. Most people are oblivious of these laws.

Yet another major law of the logic of language is not to use words that have strong emotional overtones, either positive or negative, unless such usage is warranted by the case. If it is not, then use unemotional or neutral meaning. For example: You are "stubborn" (negative or derogatory), I am "firm" (positive or laudatory) and she is "not changing her views" (neutral or unemotional).

The following are some quite negative emotional words used to describe people: "mean, nasty, selfish, greedy, pathetic, bitchy." **Using such emotional words easily biases an uncritical listener to be unable to objectively think about the facts to which they refer. The emotional overtones or connotations of words can be quite powerful. Use neutral words almost always.**

4. THINK CRITICALLY

The next main law of logic is to think critically (negatively) defined as "finding faults or weaknesses in thinking." All thinking can be criticized to some extent. The opposite thinking embodies the truth to some degree. For example, the statement "humans are good" embodies truth to some degree, but so does its opposite, "humans are bad" to some extent. **Specifying the precise extent to which opposing statements are true much helps critical thinking.**

Another main law of thinking critically is always be as specific in your thinking as you can. This makes your thinking

more concrete. **A excellent way of doing this is to give examples for any general point that you make,** for examples, give an example of respects in which humans are good (such as in helping others) and in which they are bad (such as lying if they are sure that they will not be caught). **Critical thinking can in this way become one of your attitudes which it ought to be because it sharpens your thinking overall.**

The most effective law to think critically is to question, not doubt, much that you are exposed to, especially assumptions. It is quite meaningful to question many statements. People tend to accept whatever they are exposed to unless it is outrageous, for examples, useless social distancing and wearing mouth masks to protect against the extremely tiny corona virus. This virus can easily penetrate these masks if they were airborne by someone spitting or sneezing directly on you. In incidents like the current pandemic, the media and politicians try to instill fear so that people will pay attention to them. To counteract this, you must have a critical or questioning spirit on such matters.

Critical thinking is largely directed by yourself since we find so little of it in our stupid society today with its gross self-centerness and functional illiteracy that all of us need to overcome.

Socrates did the first critical thinking in condemning the immorality, injustice and ignorance of ancient Athens where he lived. He was certainly very critical of the beliefs of practically everybody whom he encountered. **Socrates implored us to always have adequate evidence or ideas, especially when we are tempted to believe what is optimistic or flattering emotionally to ourselves. Socrates also implored us to ask deep questions**; for example, what is the good life, because such big questions make the broad foundation that guides your other beliefs and actions on this. (See Chapter 2 on "Philosophy Is Your Basic Beliefs.")

You need many mental skills to think critically. The first is to feel, not just think, the need to criticize statements. You then need to follow up by creatively thinking of other perspectives to acquire relevant alternatives. (See "Creative Thinking" in the next section.) Also, you need the mental skill to think about logic in general to arrive at sound conclusions. This is a genetic gift, but it can be much improved by frequent practice.

Yet still another law of critical thinking is to avoid fallacies or incorrect patterns of thinking, for examples, attacking the speaker personally rather than her argument and leaping to a conclusion without enough evidence in the premises.

There are literally hundreds of fallacies or ways in which thinking goes wrong. See the "Index" in my other books on making meaning for more about and examples of fallacies and logic in general.

Critical thinking ideally ought to be done before thinking creatively or constructively. A critical attitude can help your creative thinking by giving it a logical place to begin it. We need to turn to this now.

5. THINK CREATIVELY

Creative thinking involves getting new ideas, for you at least. We can also call this "creativity" or "being creative." It produces novel ideas that are often useful and valuable, especially in solving problems.

For most centuries, creative thinking referred only to God in his creating and designing the universe. Ancient Greeks and Romans thought that they could be inspired by messages from the muses or the nine goddesses who preside over the arts and sciences.

Creative thinking was not applied to humans until the Renaissance in the sixteenth century and the enlightenment in the seventeenth century. During this time, creativity was regarded as coming from the mental abilities of great men, for example, inventor and artist Leonardo da Vinci. Creative thinking is tightly linked to the imagination.

"Creative thinking" is quite hard to define and pin down, since it is constantly new. Yet, it is not necessary to strictly define such a slippery term since we now have a general idea of what it is. That is enough for this topic.

EXAMPLE OF CREATIVITY: CALDER'S MOBILE

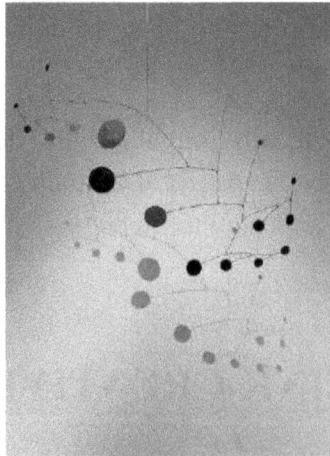

Calder, "Mobile"

An extended example of creative thinking in the arts comes from artist Alexander Calder's invention of what he called a "mobile" or moving sculpture. These now are often seen bobbing above babies' cribs. (His immobile abstract sculptures called "stabiles" occupy large public spaces in many big cities of the North in the Western Hemisphere.)

Trained as an engineer, Calder made small shapes out of thin metal. Then his creative thinking took an imaginative leap, perhaps triggered by an inspiration: he suspended these small abstract shapes from wires and he delicately balanced them. They thereby became moving or mobile because they were subject to the slightest air currents, thus allowing a free and natural play of abstract shapes. **Calder's thinking about sculpture imaginatively disconnected with his previous idea that it is static. This is the key to his creating a new form of sculpture and actually a new type of art.**

ANOTHER EXAMPLE: POLLOCK'S DRIPPINGS

Pollock, dripping

Another extended example of creative thinking in the arts comes from artist Jackson Pollock. In his paintings he dripped and splattered paint on canvases on the floor. This was a totally new type of painting in the 1940's. Borrowing from the sand-throwing artistry of Native

Americans of the Southwest, **Pollock freed his paintings from his conscious control. He let his subconscious mind take over to some extent in his dripping and splattering of paint.** His paintings look like a mess, to be sure, but so does your subconsciousness! **Pollock's drippings show creative thinking that helped open up art to the newly discovered realm of subconscious meaning.**

DE BONO'S LATERAL THINKING

Logician Edward de Bono calls his brand of creative thinking "lateral" or cutting sideways across the traditional vertical logic of premises and conclusions in arguments. (See Chapter 4 on logical arguments.) This changes to a new way of thinking for which no mechanical rules exist. He cites, but does not give examples of, the fact that **most of the major discoveries in medicine come from accidents, chance observations, mistakes and humor. Such sideways thinking switches one's mind from familiar ideas to new, unexpected ones.**

Lateral thinking aims to achieve insights by moving or even jumping across logical thinking to express many images. **The thinker should not judge her thinking at this point.** De Bono next uses what he calls "fishing questions" to open up thinking.

The goal of lateral thinking, including deciding, is to have good feelings, which is the response of a person as a whole, to think about more creative ideas, according to de Bono. We hope that we can likewise have good feelings about his ways of thinking!

To summarize lateral thinking, De Bono offers us what he calls the "Five Minute Think":

One minute: target and task

Two minutes: expand and explore

Three [two?] minutes: contract and conclude

Pablo Picasso

The pre-school years are actually the golden age of creative thinking in a person. As one of the most creative artists of all time, Pablo Picasso wrote, "I used to draw like Picasso, but it has taken me a whole lifetime to learn how to draw like a child." During childhood a young person is widely open to new ideas and inspirations.

INCUBATING CREATIVE IDEAS

Incubating or taking time to allow new ideas to develop is a key law of creative thinking. Using this, you do not become fixated on wrong solutions and misleading clues to solving a problem. **Incubating allows the subconscious part of your mind to take over while the conscious part is distracted. This allows the thinker to make new connections between her ideas without having to impose rigid logical thinking on them.**

Sleeping can aid in incubating creative thinking. R. E. M. or rapid eye movement sleep now appears to be the most productive type in which a sleeper can best recall her dreams vividly. In this state of mind, the pre-frontal cortex in the brain re-organizes ordinary thinking by complex chemical processes.

Creativity can occur during a dream. A major example: scientist Friedrich Kekule dreamed about each of six slanted snakes biting the tail of the snake in front of it. When he awoke, he used this dream to explain the configuration of benzene rings on which he had worked rationally for a long time without success. At a dinner honoring him for this, he implored, "let us learn to dream" by which he encouraged us to learn how to unlock creatively from our dream states as he himself did in the major case of benzene.

Another factor that can aid in incubating creative ideas is taking time to think in terms of positive emotions such as freedom, peace and love. This increases the number of affirmative choices available to solve a problem. (See Chapter 3 on "Making Meaning for Oneself" for a similar account.)

After incubating, a thinker ought to generate multiple solutions to a problem. Creative thinking occurs when quite different frames of reference intersect, for example, order and chaos. **Your thinking needs to be highly flexible and fluid at this stage**; for examples, raising questions such as "What if it were otherwise?" and "What else might work?' **At this point a creative thinker needs to be quite open to any possibility, as artists tend to be.**

One way to improve creative thinking is to increase one's intelligence, for the two are correlated. Although this is certainly not easy to do, **the most effective way of increasing your intelligence is, again, to read books that have substantial content.** Most people find such reading hard because they must transform printed words into abstract thoughts. However, just as reading becomes easier with practice, so does creative thinking.

Creative thinking also correlates with personal moods. We find this particularly true for artists who are well known for their intense moods such as sculptor Michelangelo, composer Robert Schumann (who died in a mental institution), writer Virginia Woolf (who drowned herself when she felt a depressive seizure coming on her) and novelist Ernest Hemingway (who shot himself dead). So, **heightening your moods can help you increase your creative thinking**--as long as they are not too negatively intense as were most of the artists just mentioned!

Similarly, creative thinking correlates with even mental diseases such as anxiety, schizophrenia and even psychosis because these allow more access to both hemispheres of the pre-frontal cortex where creative thinking originates in the brain. Vincent Van Gogh might well be an example of this. (See "Finding Meaning in Van Gogh's Night Sky" in Chapter 8.)

THE CREATIVE TYPE OF PERSONALITY

A certain type of personality thinks more creatively than do others. This type has an ability to generate diverse responses to a problem. They also are strongly dedicated to being creative in their fields. Such **motivation can come from inside a person such as her interests, hopes, goals and desires. Or motivation can come from outside a person in such forms as money, rewards and fame.**

Thomas Edison

The creative type of personality engages in much spontaneous thinking, as did automotive pioneer Henry Ford and super-inventor Thomas Edison. **This type of personality is self-confident, ambitious, impulsive, driven and dominant.** Strive to be like this to think more creatively, but this is certainly not easy.

Other people who had the creative type of personality very briefly include the following with their inventions (following "for") and their inspirations for them (following "from"):

the highly motivated Wright brothers, an unusual pairing, for the airplane from studying various gliders;

James Watts for the steam engine from previous machines;

Eli Whitney for the cotton gin from many analogies (or comparisons) to other machines;

Francis Crick for the double helix in DNA also from many analogies to designs; and

Charles Darwin for the theory of evolution from the view of the survival of the fittest.

All these major inventions were thus made with the help of something to compare them to, not from nothing. They all also resulted from the creative type of personality who relentlessly thought about them.

Creative thinking is a skill that can readily be improved by practicing it. One of the methods of doing so is to purposely provoke (distort or exaggerate) your thinking by, for example, comparing it to something very different.

Another method is taking risks to think differently. Most of these risks will be utter failures, but a few will result in new ideas for you. You need to learn to tolerate the uncertainty that accompanies thinking creatively.

AN EXAMPLE OF A CREATIVE GENIUS: MOZART

Wolfgang Amadeus Mozart

A genius in creative thinking has the trait of being extremely sensitive, especially in finding solutions to problems. She also is able to go beyond her early work and thus make creative advances. An excellent example of this is famed composer Wolfgang Amadeus Mozart--despite his obnoxious laugh in the film "Amadeus"! He wrote a letter to a friend stating that he had composed a symphony in his head, but had not yet written it down. He wrote more than six hundred pieces of music, including forty-one symphonies and forty- odd operas and masses during barely thirty years, beginning quite young. He rarely revised his works.

Mozart's creative genius conflicts much with composer Ludwig von Beethoven's sometimes painful, even tormented, agonies when he was in the throes of creating compositions. Mozart, on the other hand, proceeded in a stubborn way. He was full of surprises. As a composer of genius, he not only glorified God, but also every molecule!

Creative thinking thus differs from the logical variety in many ways. **"Anything goes" is the motto of creative thinking**. Such thinking should randomly associate ideas, not logically. Unlike the logical type of thinking, it is best practiced in solitude rather than conversation, although both types benefit from a supportive environment.

Some remarks to conclude on making meaning by creative thinking: it clearly fulfills all human thinking, according to psychologist Rollo May. He wrote that it often has brought joy to thinkers. Poet Stephen Spender similarly compared creative thinking to *"wrestling with God."* Thus, when a person thinks creatively she most resembles God as a creator, according to philosopher Etienne Gilson. He regarded creativity as an *"Inner Force"* His use of capital letters strongly implies comparing it to divine activity.

In short, when a person thinks creatively, she is totally free and her mind is sovereign according to artist Ben Shahn. Wow! Such a deal! (See Chapter 12 on how causes make it quite hard to choose freely.) Realizing all this specialness of creative thinking might help you do more of it.

Knowing how to think creatively can make huge meaning for others. For example, President John F. Kennedy had to do so to avoid an all-out nuclear war with the Soviet Union during the Cuban Missile Crisis. In 1962 Soviet ships were sending nuclear bombs to that island near the U. S. He then needed to think logically, both critically and creatively, to avoid a nuclear attack.

All of us need to do likewise for every major decision that faces us, although the stakes will not be nearly as high! (JFK's actual thinking on this crisis is too lengthy to summarize here.)

A concluding comment on this chapter on logic: All of a person's thinking is deeply affected by what is called "the personal point of view," that is, it is highly subjective and therefore quite biased toward her own experiences. We tend to be automatically quite defensive about our beliefs and experiences.

Our subjectively-biased thinking much needs to become as objective as we can make it. For factual matters, we can rely on the laws of induction and critical thinking. Likewise, we ought to strenuously apply the laws of deduction to opinions to try to attain objectivity in this highly personal and subjective area. **You much need to be constantly conscious that your thinking is deeply affected by your personal point of view. This makes it quite conservative and subjective.** These are not the goals of logical thinking.

Many of our attempts to do this will fall short. **Yet, as long as the laws of logic helps a person attain soundness which includes inductive probability and deductive validity, clarity in**

communicating and defining words, critical attitude and creativity, they can make much meaning in your thinking.

The ability to think logically is a skill that cannot be taught directly, but it can be learned by knowing about it. **Using the laws of logic will help you think well about the deep but vital issues of making meaning in all the fields of philosophy in the following chapters.**

Let's now venture into the dense jungle of making meaning in the fields of philosophy armed with the impenetrable armor of the universal laws of logic!

EXERCISES:

1. Construct one inductive argument and one deductive one.

2. Name four emotive words, both positive and negative.

3. Define one word by its genus and specific difference as Aristotle specified.

   4. Think critically about one statement that you pick.

5. Name one creative idea that you have thought of. How did you get it?

Chapter 5

MAKING MEANING BY KNOWING

The philosophy of knowing is the first and most fundamental field of philosophy because before you say what you believe, you first need to say how you know that it is true.

"Knowing" can be defined as "mentally understanding a truth." Plato defined it as "justified, true belief," but each term in his definition is problematic which I will address in this chapter.

Knowing the truth is now widely thought to occur when a person's belief corresponds to objective reality. She can justify such beliefs with reliable inductions from the external world, but she cannot do this for intangibles. Thus, defining "knowing the truth" is still ongoing because of its complexity. (In this chapter "truth" does not refer to "the opposite of telling a lie"!)

One complexity of knowing the truth, for example, is that it can be either practical or theoretical. However, practical knowing involves complex cognitive theoretical processes, for examples, perceiving and reasoning.

Another complexity of knowing is that we can know a wide variety of very different kinds of things such as physical objects, actions and events, to name a few.

Yet another main complexity of knowing is that, as skeptic David Hume wrote, every experience could be contradicted the next time. (Recall that this is also a main weakness of induction.) For example, the corona virus pandemic scared almost to death almost everyone, but mostly a small per cent of already seriously-ill died from it. Yet, many people with such pre-existing conditions did not succumb to this virus. Experience thus cannot guide our knowing without contradictions, but adding thinking or deduction often makes only a small dent in complicated matters.

Yet still another complexity for the debate on defining "knowing such a truth is surely a great good" is that we can confuse it for our dreams and other similar mental states. Philosopher Rene Descartes pointed out that during a dream, a sleeper believes that it is real. (Perhaps you are dreaming now. That would be a nightmare! Ha! Ha!) However, this complexity is rather minor and theoretical.

A final, but major, complexity in the debate on "knowing the truth" is that it is quite hard to get strong evidence (or grounds) for beliefs other than the physical. **Evidence is crucial for any claim to know. In order to be justified in believing anything, a person needs to develop sound reasons or, as Plato put it, "give an account," especially for intangible truths that involve more than physical facts**, for examples, knowing what is goodness and justice. What a person says counts little unless she can support it with adequate evidence.

SOLVING THE PROBLEM OF SKEPTICISM

These many complexities regarding knowing truths raise the problem of skepticism, defined as "doubt that we can know truths other than simple facts." Many factors indicate that we do not know much about big truths. Major limiting factors include our weak faculties for knowing, the limited scope of our knowing and the diversity of beliefs due to our abundant subjectivity and relativism. (See "Moral Relativism" in Chapter 7.)

To solve skepticism, philosophers Bertrand ("Bertie") Russell and William James advised us to **be tough-minded or highly critical regarding all claims to knowing.** (See Chapter 4 on "Think Critically.") A knower also needs to be creative to think about big truths to use as the foundation of her knowing. (See Chapter 4 on "Think Creatively.") For big beliefs, don't most people simply believe what they want to that is flattering or optimistic to them? **Simply believing in a savior God who grants us immortality with our loved ones is an obvious example of this. Aren't such people emotional cowards in not trying to know the truth? Yes!** Little could be more cowardly than living for delusions and uncriticized beliefs just to feel that one's life is meaningful. **This shows your strict need to refute skepticism to enable you to make genuine meaning by knowing.**

Name one person who lived an objectively meaningful life by living for a delusion. You (and I) cannot do so.

Your knowing truths makes much meaning or matters much to you whether you realize it or not. As philosopher Francis Bacon wrote, exaggerating only a little, **a person is but what she knows.**

A healthy, not a sick or extreme, skepticism precedes all personal--and social--growth. You must first admit that you have doubts about knowing big truths in order to need and want to know more.

The best way to solve the fundamental problem of such skepticism is by studying the philosophy of knowing. (I will indicate my solution at the end of this chapter.) In this field **you need to constantly question all your beliefs, not to totally doubt them**. Doing so guards against all fanaticisms such as blind religious faith and extreme patriotisms such as Fascism and Nazism.

As Francis Bacon asserted, "**knowledge is power**." The main way that it does so is by telling us how to do actions. This can help a person much. On the other hand, ignorance is not bliss, as people sometimes say. Instead, it can be quite harmful; for example, when you do not know about a fatal but curable disease such as a cancer that you have. Ouch!

Philosopher Mortimer Adler rightly asserted that "**truth is the greatest and highest value of the human mind.**" Be unlike skeptical Pontius Pilate who refused to judge Jesus by asking his accusers, "What is truth?" **Let's define "truth" for now as "that which corresponds to reality."**

Truth has no degrees, although knowing does. For example, acquiring philosophical beliefs broadens one's degree of knowing many deep truths, as discussed in Chapter 1. There is only one objective truth about a thing, but not our attempts at knowing it.

Knowing one intangible truth solves the problem of extreme skepticism. (See "Knowing Intangible Truths" in Chapter 6 for many examples.)

Questioning one's basic beliefs can make much meaning by opening a person up to the need to develop her own philosophy of knowing. This is another way to solve the problem of skepticism. Let's first turn to the most influential and popular one.

THE PHILOSOPHY OF KNOWING FROM EXPERIENCES

Only after a person solves the problem of extreme skepticism does she become entitled to develop a philosophy of knowing. These philosophies primarily tell us how we can know truths, especially big ones. By enabling you to know such big truths, a sound philosophy of knowing enables you to make much meaning for yourself.

We call the most popular philosophy of knowing "empiricism," but it would be clearer if we called it "experience-ism." This is the philosophy that all our knowing comes from our sensory experiences or our encounters with the world by our senses, especially seeing which gives us approximately eighty per cent of our knowledge. (This figure includes what we learn by reading.) We get our knowing of all facts from our sensory experiences. **We ought to test all our knowing by our experiences, according to this philosophy.**

Empiricism has become an implied dogma (or the correct view not to be doubted) to virtually everyone today. It is also an implied dictator of a narrow materialism. (See "Criticisms of Materialism" in Chapter 6.)

Empiricism is the simplest philosophy of knowing, but it might well over-simplify such a complex subject. It explains physical facts well. However, this simple knowledge is all that it explains adequately.

As I have emphasized, **philosophy of knowing is most meaningful when it can explain big truths that we need to know to prosper, not just facts that we need only to survive.** Why would anyone want to survive with little meaning to believe in? She would have little reason or purpose to do so.

LOCKE'S EMPIRICISM

John Locke

Empiricism is surprisingly a rather new philosophy. It started in the late eighteenth century in the writings of philosopher John Locke whose version of it I will briefly examine here to determine if it enables us to know big truths.

Locke was so interested in morals and religion that he often discussed these topics with his learned friends in his "parlor." They, like us, often had to admit skeptically that they "did not know the answers" to big questions. So, he wrote a very big book An Essay on Human Understanding using the method of "plain facts" to "inquire into the origin[al], certainty and extent of human knowledge." (He had a lively writing style!)

Locke began by contending that "we get all our knowledge from one word, experience." He likened the human mind at birth to "a blank slate on which no characters are written." However, he **had to admit that our minds do have innate (or inborn) drives** or tendencies, for examples, thinking and learning. Recent studies in genetics have confirmed this, for example, a person's tastes, as we will find out in the next philosophy of knowing (rationalism) which this supports.

Human knowing on this view starts from what Locke called "a simple idea" or getting a datum from one sense alone, for example, seeing a color like red. He maintained that a person's mind immediately abstracts from this sensation and combines it with other simple ideas to form what he called a "complex idea" or what we today call a "perception." For example, I experience by my senses something hard, cold, fist-size and white. Abstracting these sensations together, I perceive the complex idea that I have just been hit by a snowball.

Locke continued that if an idea copies, corresponds to or pictures something outside the mind then that idea is true. Empiricists contend that they can know even the idea of infinity by looking at the sky and then adding to it complex ideas such as stars and galaxies endlessly.

Likewise, she can know the idea of eternity from the simple idea of a second and then adding complex ideas about time such as minutes and hours to it endlessly.

CRITICISMS OF EMPIRICISM

Critics were quick to point out that **empiricism by appealing to our sensory experiences poorly explains our knowing big truths such as ethical goodness, God and free will because all these are not sensed at all because they are spiritual or intangible,** not things. We cannot know them by adding simple ideas together. That is too simple!

Critics further pointed out that we cannot prove that our ideas correspond to even physical things because all that a person can know according to empiricism is her sensory data, not things in themselves. **We are forever trapped inside our ideas, as Locke himself had to admit. Thus, empiricism does not satisfactorily explain the problem of extreme skepticism. Instead, it causes in this problem!**

Yet still another major criticism of empiricism is that it diminishes the power of our minds to know big truths by limiting it to the senses. Our minds often distort our sensory experiences. We have many personal biases, for example, conservative and liberal. We internally impose these on our sensations. We frequently see what we expect to see. For example, one study proved that white people claim to see guns in the hands of black men when they are really in the hands of whites, according to journalist Sydney J. Harris. (See the conclusion to Chapter 4 on the personal point of view.) **To know big truths, we need to involve our minds centrally.**

Empiricism makes our minds too passive. It conceives of them as similar to trash cans into which we toss our sensations. Such an image does not give enough dignity to the complexity of our knowing despite empiricism's popularity for knowing the facts. Again, that is all that it can explain well, but it needs to also explain big truths about our lives to make much meaning. Empiricism cannot do this.

THE PHILOSOPHY OF KNOWING OF RATIONALISM

A second major philosophy of knowing is rationalism. However, it would be clearer if we called this "reason-ism." **It holds that a person gets knowledge when she reasons or makes a mental judgment about what she is sensing. She needs to be able to comprehend or "grasp" her sensations to know them.**

Rationalists solve the problem of extreme skepticism by specifying that we can know big truths by correct thinking about them. Thinking gives us more certainty than experience which varies much. Rationalists call the human faculty of thinking about big truths "reason."

A rationalist has much faith in reason. The period of history in Europe during which society had this faith came to be known as "the Enlightenment and the Age of Reason (1615-1815)" which was a quite prosperous and progressive time. **Relying on reason can bring similar enlightening to you.**

An extended example of how we can know truths by rationalism is mathematics. We do not know this subject by experiencing or sensing things because they do not contain abstract relations such as multiplying, dividing and even large numbers like 789 as distinct from its neighboring numbers. **A person needs to think clearly and strongly enough to conceive of math to know basic operations and big numbers.**

Some critics protest that math gives us only purely abstract ideas in relationships to each other. Yet, **why does mathematics apply so well to the physical world (and many other possible worlds) if it does not contain Ideas that exist on their own for us to discover?**

This question will be further answered in the next chapter on intangibles.

Another extended example of a truth that we can know by rationalism are the basic principles of the social and natural sciences, for example, causes. Every science requires them, but they cannot be directly experienced or sensed. We do likewise in daily life when we think of model ideas which structure our experiences, for examples, the categories that we use to classify things that we experience such as humans, animals, plants and minerals. **We cannot know such truths directly from our experiences. We must process them in our minds by our thinking about our sensations.**

Recent studies in genetics have shown that our brains are "wired" from conception to learn. For example, linguist (and later a radical political philosopher) Noam Chomsky noticed that infants start speaking in sentences early in their lives. How do they know the complex structure of language and the rules of grammar unless their brains are wired to do so? This reverses the empiricism's process of knowing from outer object to inner mind. **Geneticists have recently identified remarkable genes that enable humans to speak verbal languages. This strongly supports rationalism.** It also makes sure that there will be no sorry situations such as in "Planet of the Apes" movies, which was originally written by Rod Serling.

Rene Descartes

Rationalists like Rene Descartes contend that we get meaningful knowledge by intuitions which he defined as "truths that we know purely by deep and clear reasoning." **His well-known example of an intuition is "I think, therefore I am."** As long as he is thinking, he knows that he exists. Even if an "evil genie" or the devil deceives him to think he exists when he really did not, he still has to think that he does exist for this to happen at least as a deception in the mind of the devil. **Clever, eh? Descartes thus thought that rationalism gives us meaningful truths that we cannot doubt, thus overcoming extreme skepticism.**

RATIONALIST KNOWING BY INTUITING

Rationalists like him insist that **we can know big truths by intuition defined as "the immediate grasp of a truth sheerly by reasoning." Plato defined "intuition" as "comprehending true reality by contemplating it." Intuitions bridge the subconscious part of the mind to the conscious as a sort of feeling from one's "gut." Intuition might be an instinctive way of knowing, drawing from one's cumulative knowledge leading to an enlightenment.** This will "strike the eye" as a non-factual truth, as even normally-skeptical Hume expressed the matter. He argued that **intuitions are**

spontaneous judgments that do not need the support of sensory experiences.

EXTENDED EXAMPLE OF THE GOOD

An extended example of an intuitive truth of an intangible known by the rationalism is that the good or goodness is whatever benefits most people involved in an action, for example, volunteering to serve meals at a homeless shelter. Plato conceived the good as the highest goal toward which all of us ought to strive. He equated it with an impersonal god hat formed the pre-existing chaos. For him, good is go(o)d, but it is also an upside- down question mark since we do not know what it is fully. (See Chapter 2 on "Plato's Allegory of the Cave.")

Aristotle mysteriously defined the intuition of the good as "the activity of reasoning mostly in accordance with the moral virtues." As his view of the good is quite close to Plato's, we can conclude that he would agree that the good benefits most people involved in an action.

Some rationalists, like Plato and Descartes, talk about intuition as if they are innate or inborn because we seem to always have them in us. It is as if they are "dormant" or sleep within us and we need to somehow "awaken" them, as Plato expressed the matter metaphorically. Recent studies in genetics have proven that **humans are conceived with amazing genes that enable us to, for example, speak a verbal language**. Innate ideas exist as at least as genetic tendencies or natural dispositions, for examples, learning a subject.

Thinking not based on sensory experiences is often criticized as resulting only in unprovable opinions. This is a definite danger for rationalism, especially regarding big truths. Rationalists must use much care in applying the laws of logic, especially for deduction and critical thinking, to guide and evaluate all their thinking. (See Chapter 4 on "Deduction "and "Think Critically.") Yet still again, opinions are a quite common and meaningful type of knowing. They can be judged in terms of the degree of their soundness by the laws of logic, particularly deduction. (Again, see Chapter 4 on "Deduction.")

In conclusion, human knowing of truths, especially big meaningful ones, is enormously complicated. All of us need to keep the philosophy of knowing firmly in our minds to tell how we can best know big truths. **Rationalism offers us a strong way of knowing intangible big truths** in all the fields of philosophy in the following chapters. I will now treat the deepest and hence most promising—but hardest! --field: metaphysics or the study of basic reality.

EXERCISES:

1. How do you solve the fundamental problem of extreme skepticism about knowing big truths? You can borrow from the summaries of knowing in this chapter.

2. Summarize how knowing a truth or knowing how to do something gives you power. Your use of an example could help much.

3. Discuss one opinion, not a fact, about which we make judgments about its truth or falsity.

4. Explain how you can know a big truth by empiricism. If you do not think that you can do so, explain why not.

5. Explain how you can know a big truth such as love, happiness, beauty or goodness by rationalism.

6.   Discuss one way in which humans are "wired" to think, for example, learning a language.

7.   Explain how we can know one truth by intuition.

8. Defend either experiences (or empiricism) or reason (or rationalism) as the main philosophy of knowing big truths.

Chapter 6

MAKING MEANING BY
METAPHYSICS

Let's define "metaphysics" as "the critical study of what truly— note the immediate need for the philosophy of knowing-- exists, especially nonphysical realities that we cannot sense like God, free will and the soul." Metaphysics studies what really exists as opposed to what merely appears to do so.

The physical world obviously exists, but does Plato's invisible world of objective Ideas exist? I defined these as "intangibles." Prominent examples of these include goodness, justice, freedom, free will, the soul, love, happiness, beauty and meaning. (See diagram shortly below.) **These are clearly cherished ideas that we live and die for despite how little that we know about them.** (See more on this later in this chapter.) **Metaphysics thus can make much meaning for an intelligent person because it can tell her what is real.**

What is real means or matters much because it can have much power for you such as bringing you free will, happiness and love. (Again, see more on this later in this chapter.) We have very different attitudes toward what is real versus what is unreal. We care little about the latter category, for example, falsehoods.

"Metaphysics" is the name given to Aristotle's writings published after his writings about physics. In the former he went beyond physics, treating such extremely complex entities as potentialities and the unmoved mover (his concept of God—more on this in Chapter 9 on "The Creator Argument for God").

Metaphysics is the deepest subject because it studies mon-material entities or intangibles. Studying it can thereby do much to gradually but indirectly improve your thinking ability overall, including about making meaning, by grappling with its quandaries.

The main question of metaphysics today is whether or not intangibles truly exist. Your answer to this question then composes your most fundamental beliefs.

If an idea such as God, free will or love exists in someone's mind it clearly has subjective reality to her. However, so do the **ideas of Santa Claus, the Easter Bunny and the Tooth Fairy, but they are not really real, that is, they do not exist objectively or in the external world. Subjective existence does not count nearly as much as objective reality** because it exists only in our brain.

To qualify as real, a thing or idea needs to be demon - started to exist in some objective or external way. As intangibles transcend facts, demonstrating them would be quite hard, but it can be soundly done by rigorously applying the laws of logic to them. (See Chapter Four.)

Now let's look at the two main types of metaphysics.

TYPES OF METAPHYSICS

The two main types of metaphysics concerning what is truly real are:

1) materialism which maintains that only matter in some form exists even for consciousness defined as "awareness of one's sensing and even thinking" and 2) intangibles which argue for non-material realities that cannot be touched or seen, for examples, goodness and justice, exist.

TYPE #1: MATERIALISM

This maintains that matter in some form is the only reality.

Materialists rely only on what they sense. They are strict empiricists in their philosophy of knowing. (See Chapter 5 on "Empiricism.") This leads them to deny that intangibles or anything non-physical exists. They also deny that our mental states such as awareness, thinking and feeling exist apart from our brains.

Materialists firmly maintain that all that exists and that you can know is matter in some form. They argue that even consciousness and thinking, results from chemical cells operating in a person's brain. We need to use the empirical philosophy to know all truths. These will all be facts. We can know nothing else. We can thus measure or count everything that exists, materialists maintain.

The sub-atomic particles of electrons, neutrons and protons in an atom are extremely small bits of matter. The many forms that they can take is most amazing. (See "How Some Types of Matter Behave Like Intangibles" later in this chapter.) Empiricists assert that these particles can become sensing and feeling processes in our brains. Such amazing particles of atoms can explain much reality, but can they explain all of it?

CRITICISMS OF MATERIALISM

The following three paragraphs summarize only some of the main criticisms of materialism. **Materialism is too simplistic. It is quite narrow-minded, limiting reality to what we can see or touch** For example, the extremely popular materialistic ethics holds that acquiring physical possessions is the greatest good. This also is quite narrow and shallow. (See Chapter 7 on "Ethical Standards.")

We cannot count, measure or weigh the most important matters in our lives because they are not physical things. For examples, how can we count how much we love someone and how free is a person? Proposing to quantify these and all intangibles is confused because they all are qualities of reality, not quantities of it.

Materialism turns humans into inert machines. However, living humans obviously differ much from them and even advanced computers.

Materialism cannot correctly explain what is human consciousness or awareness. Mental awareness cannot come from matter, no matter—get it? Ha! Ha! --how complex, because such **awareness is not physical at all**, although it can be aware of physical things. Even super-fast particles cannot be conscious in any way. (See "How Some Types of Matter Behave Like Intangibles" later in this chapter.)

CONSCIOUSNESS DIFFERS VERY MUCH FROM MATTER (THE BRAIN) IN THESE WAYS:

consciousness exists totally within or **inside** a person, whereas matter is outside a person;

consciousness is totally **subjective,** whereas the brain is entirely objective;

consciousness is totally **private**, whereas matter is entirely public or open to everyone;

consciousness is totally **abstract**, whereas matter is entirely concrete or physical;

consciousness is a state of mind that **can be aware of even itself,** whereas matter consists of inert atoms that have no awareness;

consciousness exists as an intangible, whereas our brains exist as slimy, soggy, gooey matter with twenty-three watts of electrical sparks; and

consciousness does not have solidity, a shape, a color or a location in space whereas matter has all these things.

Thus, matter in our brains and consciousness in our minds differ in so many ways that they appear to be two different kinds of realities, although they can overlap or meet in a person. (This philosophy is called "dualism" which refers to the fundamental two-ness of reality: matter and the spiritual or the non-material.)

EXAMPLES OF CONSCIOUS STATES THAT CANNOT COME FROM THE BRAIN (MATTER):

abstract thinking, although the cerebral cortex in the brain is active during thinking;

all truths about intangibles such as justice, goodness and beauty which are found nowhere in the brain; and

meditation and advanced mental yoga which have been proven to go beyond all brain states.

CURRENT CONCEPTIONS OF MATTER

In current quantum physics, matter has become de-materialized in revolutionary and foundational ways into mostly intangibles. We now know that there are over one hundred types of matter with over two hundred kinds of sub-atomic particles. These in turn consist of elementary particles called by the playful name "quarks" from writer James Joyce novel Finnegan's Wake. **These are more like dynamic waves than hard matter. Instead of lumps, matter is now conceived by scientists to be wildly vibrating particles held together by a mysterious force—God?** No other candidates are available!

Scientist Arthur **Eddington argued that there are really two tables in the one that we see**: 1. the sensed (seen and touched) material table which is very familiar and easily understandable and 2. the scientific table consisting of trillions of atoms with their particles in much empty space between them spinning at extremely fast speeds like waves according to current quantum physics. Which is the real table or are both real? Both! **Scientific proof that the second table exists shows that intangibles exist as well as matter.** This will be shown in the next section on the newly-discovered nature of matter.

The exact location of a piece of matter cannot be determined until it interacts with the observer, again according to current quantum physics. Has matter thereby become an intangible? Some types of it mostly are not physical. Let's look now at this matter—Ha! Ha!

HOW SOME TYPES OF MATTER BEHAVE MORE LIKE INTANGIBLES

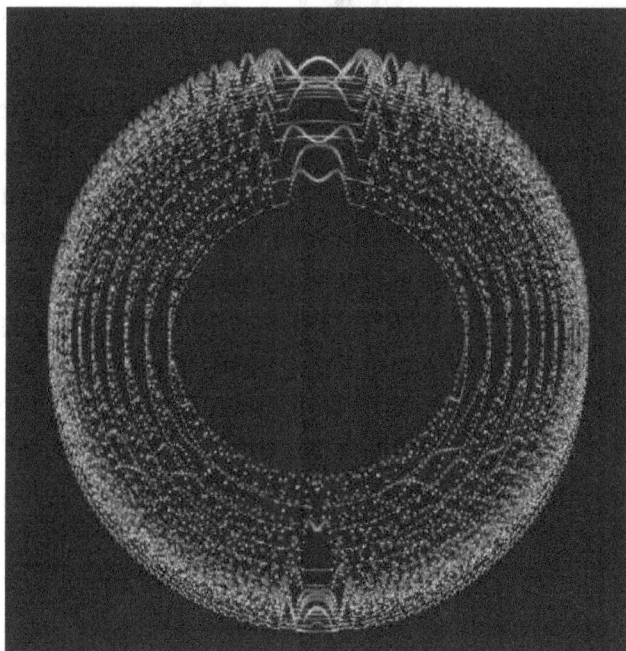

The NEUTRINO is a sub-atomic particle with no physical properties, for examples, no mass and no electrical charge. Perhaps it exists in a different type of space governed by different laws. As you read this sentence, 100,000 million neutrinos are passing through one centimeter of your body! This hardly appears to be the behavior of matter traditionally conceived as solid lumps.

The **PHOTON** is the smallest and most populous particle. It is always in motion and in a vacuum. **A stream of photons can act as both a wave and a particle. It has no mass, but it gives light. Think of a photon as a packet or bundle of energy that contains the smallest amount of energy that matter can absorb at a time. These considerations show that photons are intangibles for the most part, although they also exist as energy and light.**

The **HIGGS PARTICLE** (awarded the Nobel Prize in physics in 2012) is produced by its field being somehow excited. **It gives mass to energy, thus making matter. But what created it? God?** No other candidates are available again! **The Higgs Particle now seems more like a set of rules for the fundamental building blocks of matter. Such rules are intangible.** The Higgs Particle operates like magic making matter appear out of nothing!

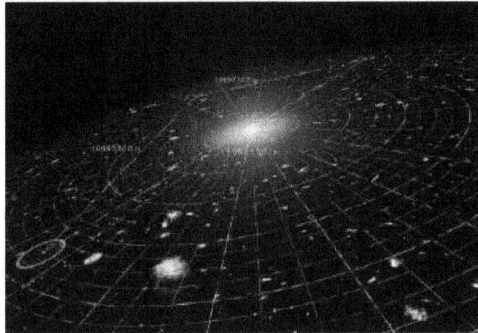

DARK ENERGY is the force that expands the universe. Galaxies are spreading away from each other at extremely fast speeds since the Big Bang. But what is the universe expanding into? This is totally unknown and mind-boggling to our puny intellects. We know very little about dark energy as an anti- gravity force, even though it makes up 68% of the universe. (Visible matter makes up only 5% while dark matter or anti-matter accounts for the remaining 27%.)

ANTI-MATTER is an extraterrestrial high-energy wave-like particle found in cosmic rays. It would destroy matter if they collided. Anti-matter has the opposite electrical charges than matter. It was created with matter at the Big Bang. Anti-matter is largely unknown now as it is so far away from us. It is yet still another type of matter that behaves more like an intangible.

Einstein at the end of his long career stated that **the universe is stranger than we can even imagine. Today his words sound even** more correct as current scientists have discovered the universe much stranger than in his time.

Such criticisms of the metaphysics of materialism as these current conceptions of matter as traditionally conceived thus are quite severe. It explains little reality except facts. We now know that even matter itself behaves mostly as an intangible, although we have much to learn about this.

TYPE OF METAPHYSICS #2: INTANGIBLES

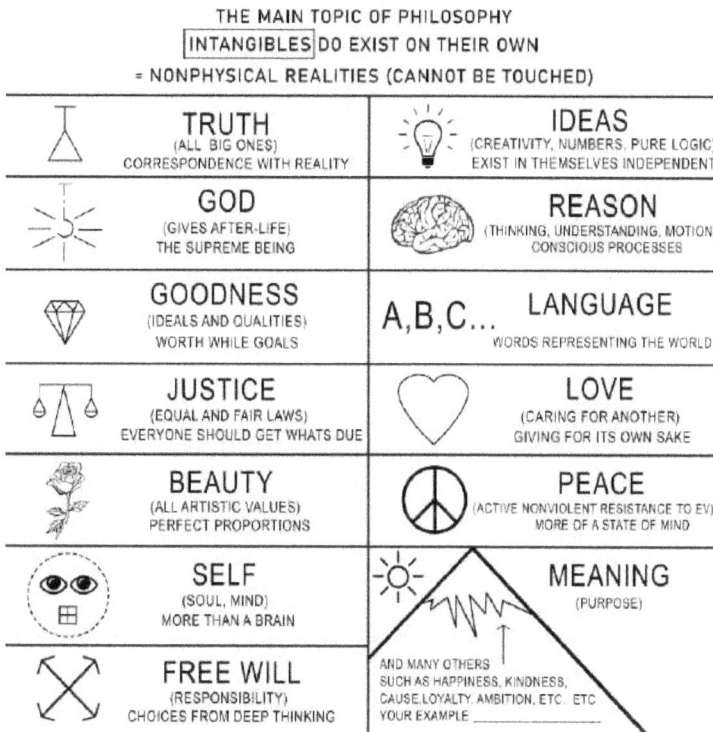

THE MAIN TOPIC OF PHILOSOPHY
INTANGIBLES DO EXIST ON THEIR OWN
= NONPHYSICAL REALITIES (CANNOT BE TOUCHED)

TRUTH (ALL BIG ONES) CORRESPONDENCE WITH REALITY	**IDEAS** (CREATIVITY, NUMBERS, PURE LOGIC) EXIST IN THEMSELVES INDEPENDENT
GOD (GIVES AFTER-LIFE) THE SUPREME BEING	**REASON** (THINKING, UNDERSTANDING, MOTION) CONSCIOUS PROCESSES
GOODNESS (IDEALS AND QUALITIES) WORTH WHILE GOALS	A,B,C... **LANGUAGE** WORDS REPRESENTING THE WORLD
JUSTICE (EQUAL AND FAIR LAWS) EVERYONE SHOULD GET WHATS DUE	**LOVE** (CARING FOR ANOTHER) GIVING FOR ITS OWN SAKE
BEAUTY (ALL ARTISTIC VALUES) PERFECT PROPORTIONS	**PEACE** (ACTIVE NONVIOLENT RESISTANCE TO EV) MORE OF A STATE OF MIND
SELF (SOUL, MIND) MORE THAN A BRAIN	**MEANING** (PURPOSE)
FREE WILL (RESPONSIBILITY) CHOICES FROM DEEP THINKING	AND MANY OTHERS SUCH AS HAPPINESS, KINDNESS, CAUSE, LOYALTY, AMBITION, ETC. ETC YOUR EXAMPLE _____

diagram of intangibles

"Intangibles," is defined as "big ideas such as goodness, justice, beauty and others exist objectively, that is, independently of our minds." In other words, this type of metaphysics holds that intangibles exist on their own or "out there," although not in any physical space. However, **intangibles such as love, goodness, justice and beauty can be embodied in humans to varying degrees.**

We do not make up intangibles in our brains. Instead, **our minds know their external existence by deep logical thinking. We "discover" intangible truths existing outside our minds**. We ought to try to know as many of these truths as we can despite how hard they are. **What can make more meaning for you than knowing truths about goodness, love, happiness, beauty, God, free will, justice and other intangibles?** What a meaningful life that would enable you to live!

I call this type of metaphysics "Modified Platonism" because it contains his belief that an invisible world of Ideas truly exists outside our brains and the cave of weak reflections of reality. (For this, see Chapter 2.) In this type of Platonism, intangible truths exist on their own in a non-material way for us to know, but they should be applied to make meaning in our daily lives, not to the abstract, as Plato tended to do.

The first task here is to give logical arguments that intangibles truly exist. This will not be simple or easy, but it is strictly required to determine if intangibles exist objectively.

EIGHT ARGUMENTS FOR THE EXISTENCE OF INTANGIBLES

Yet still again, the importance of having sound arguments or evidence to support—colloquially called "back up"--all your beliefs is hard to over-emphasize. (See Chapter 4 on "Think in Terms of Arguments.") **We need such arguments to be entitled to think that a spiritual or non-material reality truly exists. Intangibles very much expand reality and they can make much meaning, so they require sound arguments for a person to rationally believe in them. Below are eight main ones:**

1. **"ABSOLUTES" are defined as "truths that always hold without exception for all time for all people." (We can also call them "universals.") These must exist, otherwise every action would be totally relative to each person. This would be chaotic, uncertain and even dangerous. For examples, if murder or rape were considered relative to each person, some people would consider them ethical.** (Partial relativism which relates everything to its context does express a minor truth. For it, see Chapter 7 on "Ethical Relativism.") **We need absolute intangibles such as goodness and justice to guide our acting and thinking.**

There are so many absolutes in ethics (and many other fields of philosophy such as art and politics) that they often conflict with one another. For example, the quality of a woman's life conflicts with the right to life of her fetus in the issue of the ethics an abortion. **In such a conflict of absolutes, the person involved needs to determine which one makes the most meaning.** In this example, the quality of a woman's life takes precedence over the fetus' right to life mostly because it is human only in the biological, not the ethical, sense.

Recall that absolutes exist on the physical or factual level as well as the non-material or intangible, for example, the speed of light in a vacuum is 186,262 miles per second, as per what Einstein confusedly called "the theory of relativity." This theory actually revolves around this factual absolute regarding the speed of light. That's quite faaaast! (See "How Some Matter Behaves as Intangibles" in Chapter 5.)

Another example of a factual physical absolute is absolute zero: 273 degrees Centigrade or zero Kelvin or 459.67 degrees Fahrenheit below zero. At that temperature all sub-atomic particles stop moving. Brrrrrr!

Yet another example of a factual or physical absolute is absolute hot. This occurred at the Big Bang. This temperature was about ten to the forty-second power Fahrenheit. That's very hoooot! (Ha! Ha yet still again!)

Shakespeare at times, especially in <u>Macbeth</u> and <u>Hamlet</u>, and Plato, especially in <u>The Republic</u>, both regarded the physical world as a mere shadow of intangible absolutes.

2. **STANDARDS are intangibles needed to mentally measure, not count or weigh, the meaning of our actions and thinking. We need objective ways to tell how meaningful is what we do.** For example, ethics can tell the goodness of a person's actions. (See Chapter 7 on "Ethical Standards.") Also, logic gives all of us laws to know the soundness of every piece of our thinking, even opinions. (See Chapter 4 on "Think in Terms of Arguments.")

Standards give a person needed ideals of how she ought to live; for example, be as positive as is realistic in your outlooks. **We all need high standards to live by.** For instance, if a person holds high standards of truth-telling, she will not lie or deceive others. **Rarely is a standard too high**. The intangibles give us many high standards, especially   goodness   and   justice,   by   which to make this artwork meaningful to you.. Remember that the Roman Empire finally fell because it gradually held such low moral standards that it could no longer resist the onslaught of the barbarians, according to historian Edward Gibbons who wrote the first history of this empire.

3. **HIGHER LEVELS OF EXISTENCE** are found throughout reality. Many philosophers, especially Aristotle and Plato implicitly, according to historian of ideas Arthur O. Lovejoy, maintained that **there is a great chain of being (or existence) which structures reality from its lowest to highest. Every link must be filled or this chain is broken**.

This chain's hierarchy starts at the bottom end with dirt and other minerals. The middle section on this chain consists of plants and animals. The top or end section must consist of intangibles because **each level on this chain has a higher quality than the one below it.** For example, humans exist at a high level because of their ability to think abstractly. So, there must be an intangible level beyond the tangible on this chain of existence. (See the quite similar argument for the existence of God from the order of causes in Chapter 9.)

4. **HOLISM refers to the fact that a whole often has more meaning than all its parts**. For example, life cannot be made by combining the correct chemicals. Also, recall here how consciousness is more than all the gooey cells in a person's brain, as has been discussed in this chapter. **Even things like pets and memorabilia are considered to be "more than" rather than "nothing but" the sum of their parts. Likewise, reality is more than matter, not nothing but it.**

An intangible composes a whole rather than a collection or sum of its tangible parts. In other words, a whole with different qualities often emerges from its parts. Wholes frequently combine their parts like living organisms into more than themselves, as the examples in this argument illustrate.

5.   **HUMAN CONSCIOUSNESS** differs qualitatively from our brains, as has been discussed in this chapter. It must be an intangible because **it is an abstract state of mind, not a physical thing like a brain which consists of slimy, spongy and soggy stuff** (or cells). How can twenty-three watts of electricity—or any amount of it-- produce awareness and thinking? How can these states of mind come from tiny electric sparks?

A person needs a brain to be conscious, to be sure, but this is not enough (or sufficient) for thinking to occur, as scientists cannot locate it in our brains. Only intangible reality can explain our consciousness.

How can consciousness be found in our brains? Where do mind and matter meet there? We cannot answer such questions. The cerebral cortex is more active during thinking, but this cannot constitute consciousness. Many scientists have tried for many years to explain consciousness, but they have not succeeded. Experimental psychologists can explain lower-level phenomena such as lust and fear, but not the highest one of consciousness itself, especially thinking. (See the contrasts of the brain versus consciousness preceding in this chapter.)

6.   **HIGHER KNOWLEDGE** requires intangibles because our senses can give us knowledge only about physical things, as discussed in the previous chapter. **We cannot know from our senses what is ethically good, for example, because they give us only facts. We need to know an intangible truth about what is good to know what is ethical in a moral problem.**

Plato in his allegory of the cave in which we are imprisoned by our senses maintained that humans who escape do have perfect knowledge in mathematics. We can think, for example, about perfect triangles, all of which have 180 degrees. None of these exist if we draw them in the physical world because of small imperfections in our drawings. Plato argued that we can get higher and even perfect

knowledge only from intangibles or what he called external "Ideas" if we escape from the sensory cave into the higher reality of Ideas known purely by thinking. (See diagram of "Plato's Allegory of the Cave" in Chapter 2.)

Also, Plato in this allegory of the cave stated that our world and knowledge "weakly reflects" intangibles, for example, our ethics weakly reflect the intangible of goodness since humans have such limited abilities for knowing big truths. (See "Skepticism" in Chapter 5.) However, **we can progressively improve our knowing about intangibles.** For example, our knowledge about the intangible of truth of the physical reality has progressed from the false physics of Aristotle, then to the basic truths about the Earth by scientist Isaac Newton, and now to the universe by quantum physics and Einstein's theory of relativity, although no one has successfully combined these two yet in what is called a "Theory of Everything." Is it now time for improving our knowledge of the intangible of the truth about the physical reality? It certainly is as much mystery reigns there now. (See "How Matter Behaves Mostly Like Intangibles" in Chapter 5.)

Another example of how we have improved our knowing about intangibles is how society has progressed from the primitive barbarism and constant warfare in its early years to being far less war-like now since the end of World War II, even though we now have far greater weapons of mass and even total destruction. We do have many small wars in recent years, but nothing like those in previous eras.

7. **WE HAVE CONSTRAINTS ON OUR BEHAVIOR. We are constrained from doing clearly unethical actions in general such as murder, stealing and cheating. We also have positive constraints**; for example, all of us are obligated to help others who have obviously greater needs than ours, according to Professor Peter Singer. We can call positive constraints "obligations." They are   actions that we are compelled to do.

It is clearly wrong to do unethical actions, for example, poking an innocent person in the eye. Doing such an action would violate the other's dignity as a person, the respect that we owe her and her ethical goodness. All three of these are intangibles, not physical things or words. They constrain all of us. (See "Intangibles Have Power" below in this chapter.)

8. **INTANGIBLES EXIST IN THE PHYSICAL WORLD. The immediately preceding study of the following examples of sub-atomic particles determined that they behave mostly or entirely like intangibles: neutrinos, photons, the Higgs Particle, dark energy and anti-matter.** (It was also stated that the second last of these makes up 70% of the universe, but we do not now know what it is.) The reader is advised to review this quite hard topic now. **What stronger proof for the existence of intangibles (or anything) can there be than physical evidence? None.**

Also, the argument for "Absolutes" in this chapter and Chapter 5 maintains that physical absolutes exist for the speed of light, cold and heat. Again, what greater evidence can there be than the physical? Again, none.

These eight arguments for the existence of intangibles are all thus quite strong.

HOW WE LIVE MOSTLY FOR INTANGIBLES

We dedicate much of our lives to pursuing intangibles of all kinds. For example, we work mostly for self-respect rather than for money. Few people would work at a job where they were not respected, but many stay in jobs that do not pay them enough.

The main intangible for which most people live is God, of course. Many people have blind or unproven faith in God to believe that they and their loved ones will have immortal joy in Heaven. (See Chapter 9 on "Freud's Criticism of Belief in God.") Many of these people also rely on their faith in God for their moral decisions. For example, a very religious woman would prefer a life-long commitment to an unwanted child rather than spending her immortal after-life burning in Hell for aborting or killing her fetus.

The following are more examples of intangibles that we live and die for briefly explained:

All of us want a good life overall, a sense of well-being and a satisfied mind. People seek these by trying to know the intangible truths about the ethical good.

We all live for the intangible of love, defined as "giving for the other's sake because one likes her so much," especially one's parents, spouse, friends and children. Hopefully they can pass it on in future generations, but this is not part of love. It gives for its own sake to another.

All of us seek to know the intangible truths about happiness, defined as "lasting positive emotional states." (See Chapter 7 on "Happiness" for a full treatment.)

We want to be caring, defined as "showing concern and kindness about others." This can come only from a person's desires which is another intangible, although a non-rational one.

Anyone who is ill needs to cultivate positive states of mind which can do more to cure physical and mental diseases than can medications which often merely hide symptoms from the afflicted.

All of us want to choose freely. This is one of the greatest goals in the lives of people. Few people realize how strong is the argument that we are caused to do everything that we do by many external and internal forces. (See Chapter 12 on free will.)

Working for the intangible of peace prevents unjust wars that are actually mass murders. The only just wars are for self-defense of lives which have been in the minority throughout history.

Along the lines of the preceding example, **literally millions of young men gave their lives for the intangibles of freedom and justice**, sometimes mistaken (for example, freedom for blacks, especially for the U. S.).

Again, along the lines of the preceding example, the intangible of truth is mistaken in unjust or aggressive wars for nationalistic pride, racial superiority--especially for the Nazis and Fascists--, false glory, propaganda and always excessively exploiting conquered people.

Exploding a nuclear bomb

Yet still again along the lines of the preceding example, the **intangible of the love of peace, plus the fear of our total destruction, has prevented nuclear wars.** "Nukes" can quickly contaminate the entire Earth, killing all its inhabitants with radioactive fall-out.

So, we clearly live or strive mostly for intangibles, particularly in critical situations, in the ways described in the preceding surveys. The main intangibles that we most want in our lives are God (including the after-life), the good life, happiness, love and peace. These are extremely important intangibles to us. We just do not often realize this explicitly. (That is a main reason for continuing to read this book!)

Knowing truths about intangibles thus can be one's main source of making meaning for oneself.

Again, we cannot get more meaning than intangible truths about God, the after-life, love, happiness, goodness and free will. What can make more meaning to you than any one of these?

Nevertheless, intangibles are quite hard to know even after studying the eight arguments for their existence just summarized. **We need strong reasons, but not physical proof, to rationally know that an intangible truth.** So, let's next explore at some length this crucial topic of knowing intangibles.

WE CAN KNOW INTANGIBLE TRUTHS BY INTUITING THEM

It is obviously neither easy nor simple to **know (or grasp or understand) intangible truths because they are the highest type of knowing.** To know them, we need to use the highest philosophy of knowing. This goes to rationalism treated in Chapter 5. **There the highest philosophy of knowing is intuiting, defined as "one's mind immediate grasping an intangible truth (in this case) after much thinking about it." Intuiting is essentially accompanied by getting a flash (!) of insight into an enlightening truth about an intangible.** This knowing goes beyond the puny processes of reasoning. Some major thinkers such as Freud and psychologist Carl Jung argued that **intuiting delves into the subconsciousness.**

An example of an intangible truth known by intuiting is "an innocent person ought to have much value"—note how this is prescriptive. (See Chapter 2 on "Philosophy Is Prescriptive.") Another example of intuiting an intangible truth is love at first sight, but this works better for an artwork than people because of their complexity.

The most that a person can do here to predispose herself to knowing a truth about an intangible is to engage in much thinking or contemplating about it until she gets an idea that has much intensity for her, according to Jung. Then she might metaphorically "see a truth in her mind's eye" by its power, according to usually skeptical and empirical Hume. **Intuiting truths can be helpful in solving major problems according to psychologist Daniel Kahneman, for examples, business investing and law enforcement in identifying criminals.**

Perhaps intuiting draws out truths latent in a person's mind, as Plato maintained in his dialogue "Meno" in which he draws out the Pythagorean Theorem from an uneducated slave boy. (But Plato might well have asked this boy leading questions by his tone of voice!)

Plato also suggested that we can intuit a truth about an intangible by "participating" in it, that is, by one's mind somehow becoming an organic or living part of it. However, he was not satisfied with answers like "participate" and "living" because they are metaphors (implied comparisons). On the other hand, **metaphors might be a way of expressing truths like those of intangibles that transcend limited literal language.**

Martin Luther King, Jr.

An example of an intuitive thinker is civil rights activist Rev. Martin Luther King, Jr. He intuited such intangibles as equality and freedom as well as nonviolence for which he received the Nobel Peace Prize. King even intuited his own demise, but he chose to be oblivious to it. This led to him being tragically assassinated rather early in his ministry at only thirty-nine years old.

Later views of intuiting intangible truths include Freud on the pre-conscious which is a state of mind—not the brain, for him! —in which truths that are on the verge of becoming conscious after prolonged thinking about them. We can describe this as a "gut feeling" after much incubation

The main criticism with intuiting intangible truths has been that they cannot be tested. I need to briefly turn my attention to this key criticism now.

The test of an intuited intangible truth is whether or not it makes meaning, as discussed in Chapter 3. In other words, does such a truth have a positive impact to improve the quality of a person's life? An example of this can come from the intuition that "people who have been wrongfully hurt, ought to have justice restored to them." This statement can be tested as true because it does have a positive impact in the lives of people who were wrongfully hurt.

What tougher test of a truth can there be? This test is more vital by far than the other tests of the philosophy of knowing: the coherence theory that an idea is true if it agrees or does not conflict with other truths, the correspondence theory that an idea is true if it matches a thing and the American pragmatist theory that a belief is true if it works—but not vice versa. It is clearly hazardous to apply the test of making meaning of the truth of an intuition to the future because it is fundamentally unknowable. Therefore, we can best apply these tests of truth retroactively (or in the past) or to the present, not the future.

This making-meaning test of intangible truths is simply enlightened common sense. Philosophy needs always to retain close connections with this.

INTANGIBLES HAVE POWER

This power comes from energy which has intangible aspects, for examples, sub-atomic particles at extremely fast speeds. They might also get this energy from the newly discovered dark energy also treated earlier in this chapter. As Neo-Platonist philosopher Plotinus would have expressed the matter, intangibles "emanate" or flow outward from an underlying reality. **We should all try to be in touch with this emanated energy to help us make meaning.**

Even simple ideas have power. For example, reading the idea to "turn this page" has the power to make a reader do so (from <u>Life 101</u> by Peter McWilliams). Another example, although negative, is the widespread power that incorrect information about the Corona pandemic such as wearing masks and social distancing have had tremendous power over many millions of people for many months. Unfortunately, both of these did nothing to slow this pandemic. Sob!

Energy connects intangibles to tangibles in the world. All of us should try our best to use the power of intangibles, as did the following two thinkers to a high degree.

Mohatma Gandhi

Activists Mohatma Gandhi and M. L. King both testified to the "truth-to-power," defined as "a non-violent political tactic employed by dissidents against the propaganda of an oppressive government." The phrase originated from a Quaker pamphlet seeking a non-violent mode of change. It enabled both of them to do tremendous good and make much meaning. **They both created huge communities united to attain worthy social goals such as freedom from prejudice.**

Gandhi also used what he called the intangible of "soul-power," defined as "holding firmly on to truth as a form of nonviolent resistance," to almost single-handedly lead the successful non- violent campaign to free India from British exploitive colonization of that overpopulated country. He inspired such civil rights and freedom movements across the world, including the enormous one led by King in 1968 in the United States. It would be quite hard for anyone to make more meaning for others than Gandhi did by the intangible of soul-power and King by truth-to-power Other leaders who have used these include Nelson Mandela, Bishop Desmond Tutu, Vaclev Havel, the Dalai Lama and Elie Wiesel.

Other examples of non-violent freedom movements inspired by truth-to-power include filling a stadium in Estonia repeatedly to sing nationalist songs and holding hands for miles in Latvia and Lithuania to help free those countries from oppressive Soviet rule.

Intangibles thus have much power for individuals and even whole countries, indeed! What reality we can create by intuiting intangible truths!

EXERCISES:

1. Can you think of other intangibles than those treated in this chapter?

2. Which intangibles, if any, do you think are objectively real?

3. What is another contrast between consciousness and the brain?

4. Discuss an intangible truth that you know by intuiting it.

Chapter 7

MAKING MEANING BY ETHICS

The philosophical field of ethics can make much meaning because it focuses on doing good actions, especially for others. If you know about ethics, you will surely know how to make meaning by doing good actions for yourself as well. However, like all the fields of philosophy, this one is not easy to know. I will try to make it simple in this chapter.

Plato defined "ethics" as "the study of the good." However, since his time in the fourth century B. C. E., it has been limited mostly to judging our actions. The primary word used to praise someone's actions still is "good," as he specified. ("Bad" is the main word used to refer to mildly wrong actions, of course.) **A good act has elements of worthiness, excellence** (not perfection)**, caring, kindness, helpfulness and respect among other positive traits.**

So, ethics is actually quite complicated, involving many overlapping ideas to varying degrees. **"Good" is a highly relative and vague word, of course, but I will try to use it in a clear sense**, although borderline cases certainly exist.

Let's define "the ethical good" as "whatever act makes the most (positive) meaning for most people affected by it." What "makes meaning" is often fairly obvious, but some cases such as lying can be quite problematic. **What is most problematic in ethics is how a person can pro-actively do good acts for others.** This would involve giving help and time to others.

A person does not hereby qualify as ethical just by not hurting anyone or by doing nothing wrong.

Making meaning gives a subjective field as ethics a degree of objectivity because it actually makes situations have positive effects for most people in an action. This is surely objective to some extent. So, what is "ethically good" is not totally subjective and relative as it is now widely assumed to be and surely should not be.

The main task of traditional ethics has been to determine what is the greatest ethical good. This proved to be impossible in practice because of huge disagreements about what this is. Useful results? Always doing your duty? **The main task of ethics is better conceived as to critically examine standards that can guide us to the best behaviors, especially pro-active ones.**

ETHICAL STANDARDS

Ethics is totally prescriptive--see Chapter 2 on this--for it tells us what we ought to do, not what we do. (Ha! Ha again!) **It gives you standards for your moral choices**. (The word "moral" is almost synonymous with "ethical" which refers more to theoretical matters about what is good.)

The truly ethical life clearly consists in actively doing good for other people, whether they be your family, friends, fellow workers, the unfortunate or any person whatsoever. You need to be a do-gooder to be ethical!

You need high ethical standards to do good for other people. The following are examples of some such standards, mostly from religions, that you can live by:

the Golden Rule to treat others as you would have them treat you which is found in all world religions;

the Ten Commandments give us much freedom but little guidance by telling us what not to do except to properly worship God in the first three commands and to honor your parents in the fourth;

the **Beatitudes** such as "Blessed Be the Meek, for they shall inherit the Earth" and eight other blessed virtues from Jesus' "Sermon on the Mount," but these give mostly consolation rather than standards;

strongly oppose any unjust law by **civil disobedience** or directly breaking it and then protesting it from jail and court according to writer Henry David Thoreau who wrote the most individualist philosophy;

and be involved in the largest group of people—perhaps only yourself!-- with whom you can make the most positive impact or meaning.

The above are very brief examples of ethical standards. There are very many others. **You need to choose an ethical standard by which you can make the most meaning.** The higher ones are more likely to do so. Absolute ethical standards are the highest.

Let's not be picky by looking for an exception to an absolute standard to disprove it. **Even if such an absolute has an exception, it still can be a fine standard.**

Immanuel Kant

The highest ethical standard, from philosopher Immanuel Kant, revolves around always doing your duties, defined as "debts or obligations to yourself and others," for examples, to help others in general, educate yourself throughout your life and maintain your health. Kant implored us to always fulfill our duties. Doing one's duties demands highly respecting people, not using them as means to getting what you want. **Your duties command you unconditionally to do your duties to other people.** Kant called this "the categorical imperative." You cannot get higher standards than duties!

Ethical standards streamline one's particular moral choices by setting up ideals for moral actions such as not lying and not cheating, even if you are not caught. **Standards are thus your rules for being ethical**. You need these to give you moral direction to your life. You obviously ought to give them much thought.

High ethical standards can thereby make much meaning, especially for others, by compelling you to do good actions to them.

Knowing about these standards adds considerable dignity to your life compared to someone who does not know about them.

Everyone needs to be quite critical of the shallow standards of her stupid society which cares mostly about materialism. Some **major examples of bad social actions that these shallow standards bring include the following:**

enormous use of non-renewal resources such as oil and gas for our cars;

cruelty and pain to animals by eating meat; and

constant warfare (196 military involvements such as sending in troops in the short history of the U. S. with only World War II clearly a just war—see "Intangibles that We Live For" in Chapter 6).

Above all, ethical standards teach us how to live a good life. Aren't we all trying to do this? Don't we all want good friends, good jobs, good families and many more goods? Yes! (Again, see "Intangibles That We Live For" in Chapter 6 and the Exercises at the end of this chapter.)

Yet, many people blindly conform to their society to escape from the hard thinking and work that making meaning requires. (See Chapter 3 on "Escaping Escapes from Making Meaning.") Every person ought to think critically about all customary morals before she accepts any of them. (See "Think Critically" in Chapter 4 on logic.) **Again, the highest ethical life most consists of actively helping others,** not just waiting for them to ask for your help.

An ethical or good life does not consist of watching vapid videos on television or playing in an escapist way on a cell-phone as most people today do with their precious "free" time. How sad!

ETHICS AS THE CAPSTONE OF YOUR LIFE

Jane Addams

Ethics ought to be the capstone (or decorative stone fixed to the top of a bridge) of your entire education and life because it teaches a student that the greatest good is to help others. What more meaningful lesson can there be? The course in Ethics was formerly taught by the president of liberal arts colleges.

Activist Jane Addams learned how ethics is such a capstone when she attended Rockford College. She went on to write the first juvenile justice system which is still used today. She founded the Hull House in Chicago to teach immigrant children to be moral and artistic leaders in their communities. **She was thus quite pro-active in her ethics by trying to do good for others, as we all should**, not passive or minimal. In this way, **Addams lived the best life that she could for others, especially the lowest. This is how ethics became the capstone of her life, as it should for each of us.**

PERSONAL ETHICS

Ethics ought, above all, to be personal, but this has been much neglected throughout its history in favor of the social, except for Stoicism during the decline of the Roman Empire. **The main ingredients of personal ethics are the highest virtues and values such as caring and compassion.** Professor Bertrand Russell wrote in his <u>Autobiography</u> that compassion for suffering people "always brought me back to Earth" when his excellent abstract thinking drew him far away from it.

Let's define "Personal ethics" as "an individual's inner judgments about what is good to do and what is the good life."

Personal ethics struggles mightily with negative meaning or meaninglessness which pervades our lives, for examples, losses, defeats and deaths. Resolving this struggle is a daily and sometimes urgent need. Living a personally ethical life, as opposed to a conformist one, is therefore problematic.

First of all in personal ethics, a person needs to be keenly aware when she enters an ethical situation. We all need to directly confront this to fully realize that it is an opportunity for doing good and hence making meaning.

Personal ethical standards are a person's values and ideals with which she believes that she ought to live by. It is of the utmost meaningfulness for an individual to live by high ethical standards. (See just above for specifics about this.) Remember again that a main reason that the Roman Empire fell was its low moral standards according to Gibbons. **Will the U. S. do likewise now?** It already has! **The same** can happen to an individual—including you--for lacking high moral standards.

Motivate yourself to be highly personally ethical. Again, this scarcely comes from reasons or ideas because these are felt quite weakly by most people. As I have emphasized, motivation comes mostly from a person's will: she must just want to make meaning. No one can explain this on a rational basis because the will in itself is irrational or blind desire, as Plato noticed. (See "Why Be Ethical?" below.) **An effective way to motivate yourself to be highly ethical (and in general) is to combine your strong will to do so with solid ideas about how you can make meaning for others and yourself.** I myself do this is by writing books about making meaning most of every day for over thirty years. Is there a better way to make more meaning? If I knew one, I would do it!

The final major point regarding personal ethics is **that a highly moral individual can have personal enlightened ethical insights over or higher than her entire society.** Such a person can lead her society to a higher morality.

Some examples of highly moral individuals are listed below with their ethical insights higher than their entire society following her name.

Buddha: do not be attached to things or even your life because these are not lasting as is selfless union with the deity.

Antigone: insist on doing the right action—she buried her brother despite society's demands. She was to be executed for burying her dishonored brother, but she hung herself to punish foolish King Creon who had regretted his command.

Jesus: love—do not necessarily like, as M. L. King qualified--your enemies and the lowest in society, as he and the despised Good Samaritan did in his parable about him.

H. D. Thoreau: be self-reliant as this greatest American individualist did living at Walden Pond by himself;

Abraham Lincoln: all forms of uniting have much power over dividing, especially in a country;

Gandhi and Martin Luther King: be nonviolent even in opposing oppression (See "Intangibles Have Power" in Chapter 7.)—ironically, both of these pacifists were assassinated, as was Lincoln.

Albert Schweitzer: do not harm any conscious thing, although he himself extended this to any living thing, as do some members of the Jain religion. They can eat only fruits that fall off plants.

MEANINGFUL ETHICS IN DAILY LIFE

Ethics should have much meaning in our daily lives. It can tell us the good that we can do by our actions. I will first briefly discuss how all of us need this because of the many moral problems that we encounter in all major areas of our lives.

First of all, **we live in extremely stressful times complicated by rapidly expanding perplexing technology that no one can keep up with it all. We need to know what good we can have amid this stress.** Further, the traditional family has weakened and so has many other supportive agencies such as the church. In addition, in recent years we have experienced the slow decline of the economy that will become steeper after the Corona Virus Pandemic. Pathetic values are shown to young people on television and social media; for examples, much greed, selfishness, violence and sexual suggestions. **There are many other reasons that we much need ethics to guide our daily lives today.**

We have many more moral problems in all areas of our lives. I will now list (in no order) some of the main ones:

being self-centered;

being lazy, especially not developing one's potentials;

polluting the air with exhaust while using millions of years of non- renewable energy while driving your car;

breaking a law if you are not caught especially cheating and lying;

causing the death of billions of sensing animals by eating them as meat;

acquiring luxuries while many millions of people do not have their needs met, according to philosopher Peter Singer; and

not being properly attentive to others in conversations and other daily activities.

Again, these examples are only some of the main moral problems that we all encounter every day.

We also much need ethics in many ways in our daily relationships with other people for them to be sustained. Even lovers betray one another, as Shakespeare presented in many of his plays. A person can be rejected after offering even love to another. We all can be easily used and even abused in relationships. Complex questions about remaining loyal to a friend, especially concerning compatibility, can easily crush a relationship.

Making meaning can much help us in many ways to have higher ethics in our relationships. The main way is, again, that if we actively treat other people in positive ways, not only do we make meaning for them, but also, we make it for ourselves by doing so: a person almost doubles her meaning this way. (See starts of Chapters 1 and 3.) Some examples of ways in which you can treat others like this are giving time, teaching others and serving as an example or mentor.

Another main way, perhaps the main one, of being ethical by making meaning in daily relationships is, yet still again, to be pro-active in having positive impacts in them. In other words, all of us need to constantly inquire how we can do good acts for other people, not just wait for them to seek our help.

Yet another way of making meaning by taking the initiative in a relationship is to follow the Girl and Boy Scouts' slogan to "do a good turn to another person daily." They look for opportunities to help others quietly and without boasting. This reminds them that we have many ways that we can contribute to the welfare of others. Scouts go by the motto "dis, dis, dis" which translates to "do your best."

Yet still another way to make meaning for others is to follow the popular saying of "commit random acts of kindness." Originally written on a place mat, this saying inspired much making meaning around the world. Some specific ways of helping others

include the following: volunteering, visiting nursing homes where many seniors are desperately lonely and picking up litter. I myself have done the last of these daily for many years while walking my unleashed dog and reading a book!

Yahoo, Blue! You good dog, you!" I would tell my dog from a folk song.

However, we must be careful that we do not overdo this and exhaust or "burn ourselves out," as the matter is now expressed and according to Kant's practical imperative, not his better-known categorical imperative which, again, commands us to follow the Golden Rule (or do unto others as you would have them do unto you. Also, see the end of this chapter on absolutes.)

We all need to do this for the other areas of personal ethics: work, health, sex, marriage and the family. I will discuss each of these in this order. Due to lacking space, I will be able only to list the main moral problems in each area, but I can briefly indicate a few solutions by making meaning.

MAKING MEANING IN CAREERS

All of us must work at careers. There we face many moral questions and quandaries. The following are five major ones in every profession: 1. a toxic environment strictly dominated by monetary profits only, 2. unethical leadership around this, 3. sexual and racial discrimination of workers, 4. conflicting goals within a business, 5. lack of personal fulfillment in most jobs and 6. questionable use of the company's technology for personal purposes. There are many other ethical issues in one's career. Again, the professions confront us with so many moral problems that I cannot even list, much less solve, them. (However, see Exercise 1 at the end of this chapter.)

The best way to be ethical in one's career by making meaning is to regard it as serving to supply the needs of others for certain services and things, not just making money for you to survive. Yet still again, making meaning maintains that we exist not just for surviving, but for prospering like a flower.

MAKING MEANING IN HEALTH CARE

Many of us now have concerns about being treated well for our health. The following are five major moral questions in health care:

1. malpractice or the failure to bring heath to an ill person, 2. violating confidentiality, 3. unequal access to quality care, 4. physician-assisted suicide and 5. do-not-resuscitate orders. As in the case for careers, there are many moral issues in one's health that I could list, but I could not solve them here because of lack of space.

The best way to be ethical regarding human health is to try quite hard to maintain it, including mental, spiritual and life itself as long as doing so is meaningful, according to the United Nations'

World Health Organization (WHO). A person's overall well- being ought to be the ultimate concern regarding her health.

MAKING MEANING IN SEX

In the realm of sex, we similarly face a multitude of moral problems. For example, what is the main purpose of sex: reproduction, pleasure, liking or love? I argue for love (more shortly below). Other ethical problems include pre-marital sex, extra- marital and casual sex, hook-ups without commitment, one-night stands and abortion. **Sex is easily our most intimate relationship to another person and so it raises the most moral questions** even such as is it ethical to limit initiation of this activity in it to one gender? No! That is a sexist view.

The best way to make meaning in sex is to always to highly respect one's partner. This requires more than the affection asked for by "Playboy" publisher Hugh Hefner at the start of the sexual revolution enabled by the development of the female birth control pill in 1960. Sexual partners need to have more than sexual desire for each other. Humans are more than sexual animals. **Some degree of love is not too much for meaningful sex.** This applies even to masturbation, which some people jokingly refer to as "self-help." Ha! Ha!

MAKING MEANING IN MARRIAGE

The most meaningful decision that most people will make in all her relationships is "whom will I marry?" One's spouse ought to have high moral character and virtues such as being helpful, caring, kind and reasonable. Most people have a deep need for a lasting love in a marriage, yet many married couples are unhappy together today.

Getting along with another person demands constant compromise almost daily, but never of your basic values, even if these are tacit. All of us much need to work hard at getting along together. Rodney King questioned, "Can't we get along?" after he beheld the devastation wrought by his severe beating by many racist police officers in Los Angeles. **We all need to work very hard at giving in to getting along, even in marriage** where we would expect not to work hard. **It is quite hard to reconcile conflicting wills as frequently as they occur in our daily preferences.**

The institution of marriage is much troubled today, although many people still want traditional marriages. It is a partnership for raising children. Do parents have a bigger duty to their children than to themselves? Yes, **at certain times in their lives children become very dependent on their parents for their nurturing.** Divorce has quite harmful effects on children as they often feel that they are to blame for it.

MAKING MEANING IN THE FAMILY

Many married people today want to have a family, that is, children, but this has declined steeply in recent decades—due to self-centered motives? Quite probably, as these are quite common today.

Like marriage, the family is as old as humans and is found in all societies. The primary problem with the family today is that its members have much freedom to come and go. **The solution to this problem is for family members to act responsibly with their new freedom. An ethical family centers around the children** because they are its future.

An ethical parent should embody such moral virtues as highly loving, supportive, disciplinary, directive, patient, effective communicating and inspiring as a role model. See Aristotle's Ethics for an excellent treatment of the virtues.

On the other hand, **an ethical child needs to develop for her family such virtues as obedience, gratitude and respect--"** Sock it to me!" as Aretha Franklin wails. Ha! Ha! She even spells this word R-E-S-P-E-C-T because of its importance. **A child needs to be raised to embody such other virtues as autonomy, caring, altruism and ambition.**

A family will need to struggle mightily with its stupid society to incorporate any of these virtues. Sometimes society will succeed simply because of its overwhelming size. Further, society today has few supports for the family such as tax credits, low-cost childcare and health insurance and even a quality education in which students learn to love reading and writing. **Parents need to counteract society's powerful negative influence by strongly modeling making meaning on their children.**

The modern family will continue to diversify. As Tolstoy wrote, "All happy families are alike, but every unhappy family is unhappy in its own way." **Since it is quite hard for even members of the same family to get along, the reader much needs to know ethics in this vital area. Then she can create a small community of family members based on love (not power) which transforms us best** and is divine to Christians. Love best creates one's soul. (I got most of the immediately preceding ideas from a lecture that I attended 2001 at the Cultural Center in downtown Chicago.)

MAKING MEANING IN SOCIETY

We face a multitude of moral problems in our society. The following lists only some of the more prominent ones: racial prejudice, political corruption, constant unjust wars (possibly including nuclear ones which can destroy the Earth with deadly fall- out—see Chapter 6 on "How We Live for Intangibles"), exploitive capitalism and widespread narrow materialism.

If you attend to the daily news in our society, you will quickly realize how unethical it is, for examples: murders, drug abuse, racial and sexual biases, violence, senseless gang warfare, etc., etc. All of these are glorified by being featured in the media so that the masses will pay attention to them, as in the human-made pandemic of COVID-19. This was to be a chemical weapon, with the financial support of $7.5 million by the U. S., but it escaped from its lab in Wutan, China, to do much harm around the world. Society knows very little about these facts and it cares even less about them and ethics.

Very few individuals can make much meaning about the many problems in their society as a whole simply because of its huge size. Other people will try to make meaning from these problems in society, but they mostly feel frustrated by their repeated failures to make such big changes.

A worse mental state is that many people feel so overwhelmed by their own emotional problems such as disappointments, depression and anxiety that they cannot care about the meaning of anything else. How very common, but extremely sad!

You probably now feel overwhelmed by so many moral problems in every areas of your daily life: relationships, work, health, sex, marriage, the family and society as a whole. **The reason that I mentioned so many problems and suggested solutions in all the areas of daily life is to show your huge need to make as much meaning as you can in personal ethics.** I hope that this section provides a basis for the long needed and much neglected field of personal ethics.

HAPPINESS

What almost everyone says that she wants most in her life is happiness, perhaps because so many people today are depressed. We need to define this very vague word so that it is not totally relative and subjective. We have much cheapened our use of this word so that it is now extremely ambiguous. **"Happiness" no longer commonly refers to Aristotle's goal for one's entire life**. We now commonly use this word to refer "my positive feeling whenever I get whatever I want." This usage much trivializes "happiness."

Even happiness must satisfy objective standards for a person to be truly happy. These must be manifested or embodied in a person's life. **One example of such standards, given by Aristotle, is that a person develops her potentials. For him, the highest potential as uniquely human is to be rational**. (As a philosopher, he would favor his own racket. Ha! Ha!)

Other examples of potentials that we need to develop to be happy include the artistic, the social, the spiritual and even the manual. **A person needs to satisfy several of her potentials to be happy,** according to Aristotle.

Aristotle also specified that a happy person needs some degree of good luck such as being in the right place at the right time, as Forest Gump always was in the movie by that title. (So "Life is just a bunch of chocolates" to him!) Most people do not have much of either good or bad luck.

Finally, **Aristotle requires a happy person to reach several of her major goals in her life** such as fulfilling or rewarding work, fine friends, contributing to society (not his examples).

Other philosophers have given us objective standards to **define "happiness." In several dialogues on this topic, Plato, like Aristotle, emphasized that happiness consists of having many virtues**, defined as "strong personality traits," such as helpfulness and truth-telling to get a sense of lasting well-being. To get this, a person needs to aim at excellence, not perfection, in performing her proper functions such as courage and kindness. A happy person also needs to have the requisite skills and dispositions to attain it. However, Plato concluded that happiness, like every other complicated idea, is a mystery in the end! Aristotle's views on happiness are fuller and more insightful.

THOMAS AQUINAS

Thomas Aquinas, the greatest philosopher and theologian of the middle ages, defined **"happiness" as "having all that a person desires."** However, since some of our desires are bad and some of them are never satisfied finally (for examples, food, sex and making money), our happiness on Earth is limited. We can be fully happy only in Heaven where we will have what Aquinas called "the beatific vision" or "seeing" God and learning divine truths in eternity. (Not philosophical ones which are more fun? Ha! Ha!) In this way a person will satisfy all her worthy desires, according to Aquinas. However, his view is quite religious depending on faith in God, not logical and rational philosophy.

Contemporary views of happiness tend to be mostly psychological (descriptive) rather than philosophical (prescriptive). (See Chapter 2 on "Philosophy Is Prescriptive.") **The psychological view regards it as lasting positive states of mind—shades of Aristotle! --consisting of what it calls "happiness-producers,"** for examples: adjusting--mostly lowering! --expectations, social supports—claimed to be 70% of happiness--, having a loving spouse and family, working at a fulfilling job, dedicating to worthy social causes, having satisfying sex, getting recognition, having control over one's life and even getting proper diet and exercise. Presumably, **if you had enough of these happiness-producers—how many? --, you could be described as "happy."**

Some current philosophers hold that happiness is prescriptive because it is an intangible. (See the Chapter 6 on "Intangibles.") They hold that we can justify such standards for happiness by sound logical thinking, For example, a person will be happy if she embodies an intangible, especially truths about what is good. (See "Intangibles" in Chapter 6.)

Ask yourself: will I be happy if I only make much money and am married with children? Will this be enough? Each person needs to think hard and long about how to be happy. Most people do that now, but they need to be enlightened by the new idea of making meaning. Don't you most need to do make meaning to be truly happy? **The more meaning that you make, the happier that you will be.**

CRITICISMS OF HAPPINESS

Happiness as the great goal of a person's life has recently been criticized on several grounds. **First, it is criticized as self-centered in that it focuses only on oneself. It is so, indeed. To be happy, a person needs to try to make other people happy by making meaning for them**, starting with her friends and family but hopefully extending further than that.

Another criticism of happiness as the great goal of one's life is that it is too optimistic. Life on this overpopulated planet has certainly been a hard struggle for most of its inhabitants. **Aren't the lives of most people full of much meaninglessness and misery such as unfulfilling work, poor relationships and the inexorable deaths of loved ones such as terrific parents?** Many people feel as if they are "sliding down the razor blade of life" (Ha! Ha!), as satirist Tom Lehrer put it. Many people, like righteous Job in Chapter 9, might well wonder why they were born, and even wish that they were not because that would be better for them.

So, is **happiness overrated, as a recent book by that title claims? Yes, for the criticisms of its being self-centered and overly-optimistic. All of us ought to aim more at making meaning instead**, as that book rightly maintains, because it does not have those reasons.

You need to have a constant supply of making-meaning projects throughout your adult life to live a happy life. These projects need to be primarily directed toward making meaning for other people. This is not easy music to listen to, but it is quite beautiful, harmonious and rewarding.

So, I **define "happiness" a person's long-lasting state in which she makes much meaning, develops some of her potentials (especially the social one), attains several of her major goals, has some good luck and has meaning-making projects for others throughout her adult life."** This is a big part of ethics. As Aristotle stated at the start of this section, all people desire most to be happy.

WHY BE ETHICAL?

Temptations to act unethically, in particular if you are not caught or punished, can be quite hard to resist because they result in free things and more free time for you. For example, suppose that you can get an expensive cell-phone if you steal it with no fear of getting caught. Why be ethical and not steal this phone?

Plato told the story of the Ring of Gyges. Wearing a ring that he found made him invisible and thus free to commit unethical acts such as stealing and killing the king to marry the queen. Gyges then felt quite happy being unethical as the king!

Many people would not wear this ring because they fear the huge power that it would give them to do evil acts. Would you wear the Ring of Gyges? You would if you did not fear its power.

All of us need to answer the question "Why should I be ethical?" The following are the soundest answers according to the laws of logic in the history of ethics.

Leo Tolstoy

The soundest argument to be ethical is that people who act unethically thereby lose intangibles, for examples, justice, goodness, respect (particularly for themselves) and especially love (also particularly for themselves). (See Chapter 5 on "Intangibles.")

Intangibles, not selfish wants and possessions, are our most meaningful needs, as writer Leo Tolstoy strongly implied in his novella, <u>The Death of Ivan Ilyich</u>. This character dies psycho-somatically—his body dies because his soul has become dead. Ivan had followed with much success only what his stupid, shallow society wanted. Ivan **Ilyich finally admits that he "had lived all wrong" by not living for the intangible of love, especially for his wife, children and God**. Admitting this just before his death saved him from Hell according to Christian belief at the very end of this short novel.

Another strong argument for being ethical comes from Plato when he answers his question about the Ring of Gyges in his long dialogue, <u>The Republic</u>. **There he brilliantly maintained that a person acting unethically enables her will and emotions to dominate her reason. This will lead her self to become unbalanced and basically out of control without the guidance of reason. Plato called such a self "sick."** It will gradually die or destroy itself by its unethical behavior over an extended period of time. He strongly implied that **hurting others by being unethical actually also hurts yourself more.**

On the other hand, if you are ethical (and do not steal the cell-phone), you are governed by reason which alone enables humans to know what is good (and other truths). Your will and emotions will follow along with what reason knows. This leads to a balanced, controlled self. Plato called such a self "healthy." So, according to him, **being ethical is like preferring being healthy to being sick.**

Plato on "Why should I (and society) be ethical?": to be balanced,

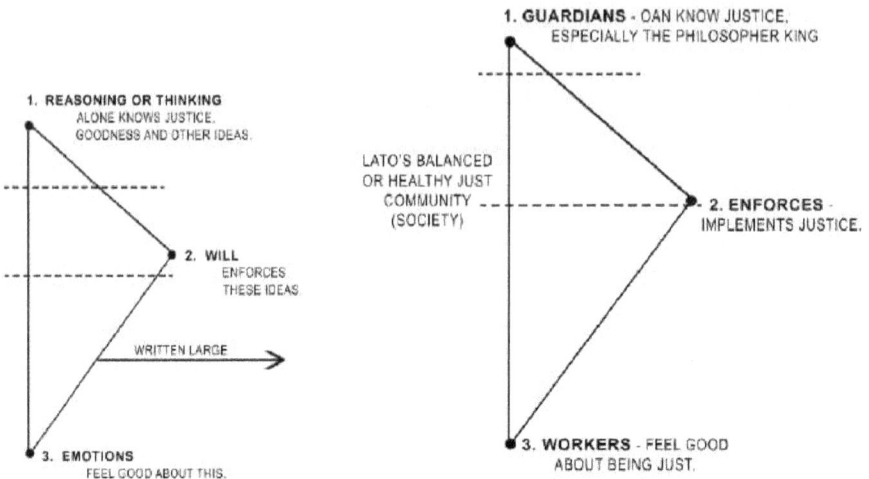

1. GUARDIANS - OAN KNOW JUSTICE, ESPECIALLY THE PHILOSOPHER KING

1. REASONING OR THINKING ALONE KNOWS JUSTICE, GOODNESS AND OTHER IDEAS.

LATO'S BALANCED OR HEALTHY JUST COMMUNITY (SOCIETY)

2. ENFORCES - IMPLEMENTS JUSTICE.

2. WILL ENFORCES THESE IDEAS

WRITTEN LARGE

3. EMOTIONS FEEL GOOD ABOUT THIS.

3. WORKERS - FEEL GOOD ABOUT BEING JUST.

healthy and ruled by reason.

Plato cleverly applied this argument to society which he likened to a collection of individuals "written large." People in whom reason rules or dominates ought to belong in the ruling or governing class. This culminates in the philosopher-king who is the wisest person. (See Chapter 2 on "Plato on Wisdom.") Those people in whom the will dominates ought to belong in the military class because they have strong will power to carry out the commands that the rulers give them, not to reason about their justice. Finally, those people in whom the emotions dominate should belong in the large business class or what he then called "tradesmen."

If the last two classes dominate, the society or country will be unbalanced and what Plato called "sick." **Like an unethical individual, an unethical society will destroy itself over time. An ethical society ruled by a philosopher-king will be healthy. It will prosper, like an ethical individual. What greater reason can there be for acting ethically?** None that I can conceive of.

Yet another argument for acting ethically is the weakest. It maintains that, as the saying puts it, "what goes around, comes around." If you treat others unethically, they will treat you likewise. Eastern philosophers, particularly in Hinduism, call this the law of "Karma." They extend even beyond the death of a person to her being re-incarnated according to the morality of her previous life. (Plato sometimes expressed a similar argument. See Chapter 5 on knowing innate ideas.) However, there is very little evidence of any kind that the Karmic view of why be ethical is true.

Plato's argument that being ethical leads to prosperity and health and Tolstoy's argument that acting unethically loses intangibles, especially love, show that acting ethically can make much meaning whereas acting unethically does not.

PUTTING "TEETH" IN ETHICS

All your personal ethics need to have metaphorical "teeth to bite" a moral problem so that you will actually do what you know to be good. To get this "bite" you need first to be aware that a moral situation or problem involves the question regarding what is good in one's life. (See "Personal Ethics" preceding this section in this chapter.) **Then try to be in touch emotionally—I have emphasized this as the strongest factor in humans--with the power of the good** to overcome the gap between knowing what is good and actually doing it. (See Chapter 6 on "Intangibles Have Power.")

Huckleberry Finn

Another way to connect concretely like this is to engage in what I call "flesh-and-blood thinking." This involves regarding abstract ethical ideas as people. For example, writer Mark Twain's character **Huckleberry Finn finally enters a firm ethical relationship with run-away slave Jim when the former person finally regards the latter as someone who has very similar needs and goals, namely, for freedom from oppressive people** such as Huck's Aunt Sally and Jim's owner on a plantation. Huck finally regards Jim as a good person and his close companion. They then work together toward their common goal of freedom—which they do not attain--by using flesh-and-blood type of thinking.

Yet still another way to put metaphorical "teeth" into being ethical comes from what Gandhi and later King called "soul force." This emanates or manifests spiritually in ethical actions, as both men achieved to a very large scale in the reforms that they brought about. Both men acted ethically to make much meaning for other people even in view of how unethically they themselves were treated "(See "Intangibles Have Power" in Chapter 6). **Soul-force, like Tolstoy's intangible of love, Plato's being rational and Twain's flesh-and-blood thinking, thus puts more "teeth" to bite into ethical problems to make more meaning in them.**

ETHICAL DILEMMAS

Often ethical problems come in the form of a dilemma. This is a decision that a person must make between two unpleasant or bad alternatives. **In a dilemma you need to forgo a greater evil to a lesser one. In general, when two bad choices conflict, it is ethical to do the lesser one. This can include acts that are usually unethical;** for example, lying to a would-be murderer about the whereabouts of your innocent friend. In this case, the good of truth- telling conflicts with that of saving the life of your friend. Lying is clearly quite ethical in this dilemma, as it would be about lying to the Nazis about concealing Jews in your attic.

All of us need to determine by logical thinking—see Chapter 4 on logic--what is the least bad in each moral dilemma that we encounter. Then we need to act on it to avoid a bigger bad from occurring. In this way you can make the most meaning in ethical dilemmas.

ETHICAL RELATIVISM VERSUS ABSOLUTES

The biggest obstacle to making meaning in ethics is relativism, defined as "the ethics of an act depends totally on each individual's opinion." Whether or not an action such as abortion or extra-marital sex is ethical varies much from person to person. Relativists say such cliches as "what is good for me might not be good for you and" "who is to say what is right or wrong?" **Almost everyone today is an ethical relativist, probably because so few people today have any explicit moral principles that they live by. Very sad!**

It is hard to know where to begin with the many criticisms of ethical relativism. **The main shortcoming of such relativism is that it makes ethical judgments, even obvious ones such as "murder is wrong" impossible to know** in a definite way. Nor can we say that one act is morally worse than another, for example, that rape is worse than cheating at cards. **What if a rapist disagrees with you? Who is right? Who wins? No one does according to relativism, because ethics is totally relative. That's obviously absurd!** There are many other severe criticisms of ethical relativism, but these are clearly enough!

Extreme relativism is wrong that all opinions are equally true. I have emphasized that the laws of logic can tell us the strength of an opinion. This is very important because **opinions are where "the rubber meets the road" in our daily lives.**

Nevertheless, relativism does contain a minor moral truth, namely, **each ethical question should be answered relative to the situation in which it occurs.** However, when this is done the action needs to be judged in terms of firm principles, ideally absolutes.

Let's define an "ethical absolute" as "a moral rule that holds for all people in all societies at all times." It thus has no exceptions. (Philosophers also call this a "universal.") (For more on absolutes, see the start of "Making Meaning in General" in Chapter 3 and "The Laws of Logic" in Chapter 4.)

Examples of ethical absolutes are prescriptive. They include the following:

1. Everyone ought to **consider the main factors of a moral problem.**

2. Everyone ought to **care about what is ethical,** defined as "what makes most (positive) meaning for most people involved in a situation."

3. Everyone ought to **make as much meaning, especially moral, as she can**, although this is quite hard and frustrating.

4. Everyone ought to **be as free to as she can.** (See the end of Chapter 12 on how to do this.)

5. **Everyone ought to help others as much as she can without over-extending or "burning herself out."** (This is what Kant called "the practical imperative" which is a version of what he called "the categorical imperative" or Golden Rule to treat others the way that you want to be treated.) (See "Ethical Standards" preceding in this chapter.)

6. Everyone ought to try to **maintain the proper balance in nature** between humans, animals, plants, soil, water and air.

You can make much meaning for yourself by knowing ethical absolutes because they enable you to act on firm principles regarding what is good. **Using these absolutes can make much meaning for all major moral decisions in your life and those that affect others.** What better way can there be, almost by definition? Name one! I cannot.

Recall the following examples of factual absolutes: Einstein's speed of light (186,262 miles per second), absolute hot (at the Big Bang) and absolute cold (when all sub-atomic particles stop moving.) (See the first "Arguments for the Existence of Intangibles" in Chapter 5.)

EXERCISES:

1. Name one good that you are searching for in your life that was not mentioned in this chapter.

2. Describe what will be an ethically good life for you as fully as you can.

3. Name some other ethical issue in the fields of careers and health care than the ones mentioned in this chapter.

4. Discuss some ways to cultivate a good or ethical marriage, for example, to develop common interests.

5. Write one virtue (or ethical character trait) that an ethical parent and a child should have.

6. Describe three main happiness-producers for you.

7. Name your three main moral values.

8. Name one example of a moral problem not mentioned in this chapter in each of the following areas of personal ethics: daily life, relationships, careers (especially health care), sex, marriage, the family and society.

9. Suggest a solution to each of the moral problems you named in 8 above by making meaning.

10. Write your two main ethical standards.

11. Describe one way to put "teeth to bite" moral problems not treated in this chapter.

12. Summarize one moral dilemma that you faced in your life and how you resolved it.

13. Name one ethical absolute not mentioned in this chapter.

Chapter 8

MAKING MEANING BY THE PHILOSOPHY OF ART

Art can be a terrific source of making meaning and even joy. However, most people get no meaning from or even experience of art. What an awful loss! Terrible! This chapter will try to restore this loss by explaining how you can make your experiences of art meaningful.

"What does this artwork mean?" is an excellent question to ask because it directs you to think about what is important in it, namely, its impact or meaning on you. You probably will need to answer this question yourself, as artists themselves are unlikely to do so for you, although they very probably could say something enlightening about their artworks, for example, why they created it.

Let's define "an artwork" as "a piece of matter formed (or shaped) to creatively express emotions and sometimes big truths." So this chapter will treat the so-called "fine arts," especially painting because it is the most visual art.

Art clearly is the most subjective field of philosophy. Subjectivity is often derided in studies, but how can a person ever escape it? We are always in our thinking and feeling. Embrace art as having much meaning because it is so subjective.

I will now explain four ways to experience artworks to make meaning for you.

1) **The best way is to interpret, that is, to explain, a meaning of an artwork. To do this, you must first know something enlightening about it.** For this you can learn about an artwork in such sources as reading about the artist's statements about it, her intentions, the artwork's school or style, its place in art history, writings about it, reviews of it and any fruitful facts about it.

Secondly, use your imagination on the artwork with this knowledge to think about meanings that the artwork can have for you. The richness of an artwork often suggests much with a little knowledge about it. Unlike ideas which are limited by their opposites (for example, good by bad), the imagination has no limits except to make an image. Although much interpretation comes from the imagination, this can feel almost as real and meaningful as your experiences themselves.

Interpreting an artwork thus involves having some knowledge about it and then imaging what this could mean. **All such interpretations are welcome as making an artwork meaningful for the interpreter. However, those interpretations that most focus on an artwork itself, knowing much about it and much imagining about it are the best.**

An interpreted artwork can have much meaning to you because it articulates in words what it emotionally signifies. **If you can interpret an artwork, you will get much more meaning out of it than practically everybody else.** We see and hear almost no interpreting of artworks anywhere even, for example, on radio stations that play difficult- to- understand classical music all day. A person who is genetically gifted with much imagination tends to favor making meaning by art since it involves much of this.

Picasso, "Guernica"

For an extended example, I will interpret Pablo Picasso's painting "Guernica" as a powerful and visceral, yet highly abstract, depiction of the horrors of war. I made this interpretation by first getting knowledge about this painting. This knowledge consists of the following which comes from just looking at the painting and knowing about it: a screaming mother holding her dead baby in a pieta pose (Mary holding the crucified Christ), the front part of a bull symbolizing Spain where the cruel bombing by dictator General Franco of the town of Guernica took place in 1937. A viewer of this painting can also see a shard of glass, a glaring light bulb, dismemberments and a gored frightened horse, broken weapons, burning buildings and screaming bodies abounding.

Secondly, I combined this knowledge about "Guernica" with a little imaging to interpret this painting as powerfully protesting the utter horrors of an actual war, a relentless bombing of civilians, that Picasso learned about.

Vermeer, "The Milkmaid"

We can interpret some artworks as better than the physical world, for examples, Utopian novels such as by Thomas More. Such artworks can make more meaning than our world does. For another example (immediately above), Jan Vermeer's sun-lit, tranquil domestic paintings draw their viewers into lovely kitchens in which you can almost hear the water pouring.

The following very briefly interprets various artworks for some of their meanings:

much music from the Renaissance sounds bold with many horn instruments such as bugles blaring just as that era was bold in its liberating thinking;

many vibrant Impressionist paintings show the people of France as quite happy with the gentle pace of their lives at that time around the turn of the twentieth century;

painter Andy Warhol's "Campbell Soup Cans" and "Coca Cola Bottles" confront us with how totally materialistic, but empty, the U. S. has become after World War II; and

"Dancing Shiva"

the above sculpture of the dancing Hindu god/goddess Shiva with many arms suggests the deity's powers such as creating, preserving and destroying the illusion of the universe in an endless circle of fire (which is poorly imitated).

2) **A second way where you can make experiencing an artwork meaningful for you involves sheerly sensing it or, in other words, focusing on only what you sense, usually see, in it.** Just sensing such aspects of your favorite artwork as its novelty, unusual shapes, haunting sounds or bold forms can be quite meaningful for you.

Sheer sensing can be done on an artwork's very materials such as the subtle colors in a painting, the striking words in a poem or the graceful and delicate bodily movements in a ballet such as Tchaikovsky's "Swan Lake."

Rembrandt, "Syndics of the Cloth"

You can experience or get much meaning in artworks by sheerly sensing them for their own sakes. For this, you usually use your higher senses of seeing (for the visual arts of painting and sculpture) and hearing (for music) in particular. For example, the gorgeous browns and reds in Rembrandt's painting "Syndics of the Cloth" (immediately above) and the different expressions on the faces of the first businessmen as you walk into their meeting can be sheerly sensed to get much meaning.

Other examples of sheerly sensing artworks are perceiving the seemingly soft skin in the sculptures made of hard marble by Michelangelo such as "David" (shortly below) and hearing the richly layered notes in a symphony by Mozart.

Even such simple designs in the interlocking L's of the Hindus, which the Nazis adapted into the horrible Swastika, **"hold one's attention to the expanse it adorns,"** according to Professor Suzanne K. Langer. She also wrote that "**the effect of good decoration** somehow makes a surface more visible," as do tattoos on a human body, for instance.

3) **A third way to experience an artwork as making meaning to you is to suspend your practical activities and mundane chores.** This can feel like a great relief from your tedious troubles. **Time also can be suspended when a person experiences an artwork as meaningful.** This is evidenced in the aphorism from Greek physician Hippocrates, "Life is short, art is long." This saying attests to the centuries-long impacts of some artworks versus the brevity of all our lives.

Gothic cathedral

A work of architecture seems like an exception because it is practical: we live, work, worship and so on in buildings. However, whenever a person focuses on sheerly sensing a Gothic cathedral, for its glory, majesty, beauty and such qualities, she is **not using this cathedral as practical thing to be manipulated, but as an artwork that she sheerly senses for its own sake.**

4) **A fourth way to experience an artwork as meaningful is to be aware of the creativity that abounds in it. Artworks actually create**

new feelings, ideas and objects. This goes beyond even the imagination, which makes different images from something.

5)   **Artworks create many new feelings in perceivers**; for example, music in the Renaissance expresses feelings of the fun of enjoying it for its own sake rather than serving God which is all that it did in the Middle Ages. (See "The Main Meaning of Art Is Emotional" shortly below.) I discuss shortly below how Langston Hughes' "Harlem," the Chicago Picasso Sculpture and Beethoven's "Ninth Symphony" create big truths. Artists are so creative that they have recently invented new artistic forms, for examples, the collage (a piece combining painting, photos, newspaper clippings and the like), Calder's mobiles (above in Chapter 4) and the new genre of science fiction writing.

One common method for being creative is to combine two unrelated images. Another such method involves fitting parts into a whole, like fitting together the pieces of a jigsaw puzzle. (See Chapter 4 on "Think Creatively" for many more such methods.) **Anyone who has ever solved a problem is creative** because she has thought of a new idea to overcome its blockage.

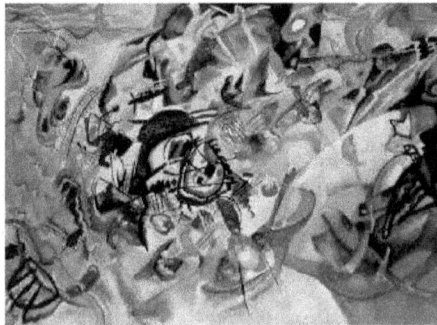

Kandinsky "Composition"

A warning about creativity in the arts: **the first time that a creative feeling or truth is expressed is meaningful because this can even be revolutionary or at least innovative**, for example, the first all- abstract painting by Wassily Kandinsky in 1913. However, the **second time that this is done has much less meaning**; for example, the all-black paintings that many painters today somehow feel obligated to make. Clas Oldenburg's numerous super-large pieces of furniture is another example. We learned from his first piece his minor point that a change in the size of an object to super-large slightly alters our reactions to it. His later works also make very little meaning.

Another warning about creativity in the arts: **It is best when novel artworks express meaningful emotions and truths, not just newness for is own sake.** For example, of a meaningful truth, Marcel Proust's serial novel In Search of Lost Time teaches us for the first time the valuable lesson that novels do not need to treat events in chronological order, just as we do not do so when we recollect the past and project to the future in the present.

To summarize this long section: you can experience an artwork to make meaning for you by 1) interpreting or explaining it, 2) sheerly sensing it, 3) suspending your practical activities and sense of time and 4) finding meaningful creative aspects in it.

THE MAIN MEANING OF ARTWORKS IS EMOTIONAL

The main meaning of an artwork resides in its expressing emotions or feelings, not ideas. This is by far the greatest impact of artworks. The emotions expressed by artworks range from the greatest joys to deepest sorrows, with countless grades between these. However, we find it quite hard to name the emotions expressed in an artwork because they are not things or even ideas.

Artworks often give us clues about the emotions that they express. For examples, fast classical music sounds lively and thus happy, whereas slow music sounds sad, for examples, "Taps" (played at the burial of soldiers) and Mozart's sorrowful "Requiem Mass" (for his domineering father). Examples of happy-sounding fast classical music include composer Edgar Elgar's "Pomp and Circumstance" (usually played at graduations) and the I-beat-the-world march in the

final movement in "The Fifth Symphony" by Tchaikovsky.

Artworks such as classical music which have no words can make much meaning for people because they express emotions that do not need to be intellectually analyzed, only felt. The emotions are the level on which we live, not ideas despite our pretensions to be rational. Almost all people consider ideas quite cold, hard and dry. Students commonly call them "boring." We soon drift away from them, whereas **we often find emotions exciting and engaging**.

Words are very poor at conveying an emotion because they are abstract, general and felt weakly. **Emotions, on the other hand, are concrete, particular—indeed, unique--and felt strongly.**

Langer wrote that, **"the [visual] arts look like our feelings feel."** Artworks express emotions quite well. This is surely not easy to do.

Artworks can express emotions in very precise ways, according to composer Aaron Copland. He wrote that, for example, a sonata can sound sad in general, but also it can sound sad in a pessimistic, resigned and many other precise varieties of sadness.

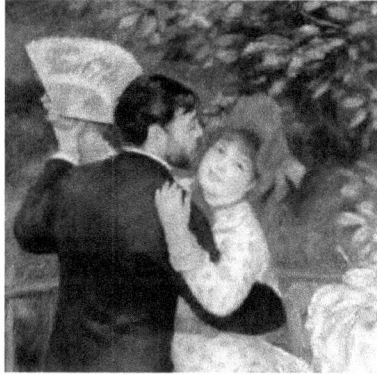

Renoir, "A Dance in the Country"

An example of a painting that illustrates how an artwork expresses emotions in precise ways can come from painter Pierre **Renoir's "A Dance in the Country." This painting expresses well the emotion of gentle love that the dancing couple feels for each other, the dance, the music, the summer night, the outdoors, the food and drinks on the table and life in general.** How can anyone ask for a more precise emotion than the gentle love that Renoir expressed in this painting?

The following are some pieces of classical music interpreted for the main emotion that each expresses:

"Thus Spoke Zarathustra" by Richard Strauss primarily expresses the feeling of dramatically arising to a higher level of enlightenment and hence power;

"Fanfare for the Common Man" by Aaron Copland primarily expresses the feeling of an average person overcoming obstacles and attaining victories in her life; and

"Messiah!" or the "Alleluia! Chorus" by Georg Frederick Handel expresses spiritual joy in the divine birth and resurrection of Jesus.

The theme of da-da-da-dah in Beethoven's "Symphony #5" sounds like "Fate [death] knocking at the door," as he wrote.

DESOLATE EMOTIONS: "NIGHTHAWKS"

Hopper, "Nighthawks"

An extended example of a painting that expresses emotions, specifically desolate loneliness, terrifically well is Edward Hopper's "Nighthawks." This greasy-spoon diner cuts through the dark night in a city under shattered but glaring fluorescent lights. Dreary insomniacs at the counter are actually isolated from each other except for the prostitute in a low-cut scarlet dress sitting on a stool next to a smoking Bogart-type detective wearing a fedora hat.

The dark street outside the diner is eerily empty and deserted. The emotions expressed in such a desolate place can hardly be uplifting.

When "Nighthawks" was painted, the residents of American cities felt paranoid after the surprise attack by the Japanese on Pearl Harbor in 1941 led to frequent drills.

"Nighthawks" expresses well meaningful emotions, especially desolate loneliness, prevalent at the time in U. S. cities. These emotions still much need to be dealt with there for such current events as the unhelpful social distancing and lock-downs following the COVID-19 pandemic. Thus, "Nighthawks" today makes much emotional meaning, even if it is negative, for both individual viewers and society as a whole.

HAUNTING ANXIETY: "THE SCREAM"

Munch, "The Scream"

Another extended example of a painting that expresses negative emotions spectacularly well is Edvard **Munch's "The Scream." This painting of a skull-like face held by bony hands screams from the horrible anxiety that today afflicts almost everyone as part of the human condition in a world with no shortage of meaninglessness.** We can compare "The Scream" to Da Vinci's portrait of "Mona Lisa" as reflecting our constantly declining times. Oh, woe is us!

Munch described how he was walking at sunset when the sky turned "blood red." This unsettling effect for him may have been due to his sister's recent commitment to a nearby insane asylum. A pleasant walk at dusk for him thus turned into his panic attack from troubling anxiety. He clearly feels overwhelmed by his anxious internal struggle. His two companions walk ahead oblivious to his desperate inner turmoil.

The haunting emotion of anxiety expressed well in "The Scream" is entirely negative, but it is still quite widespread and much needs to be dealt with today to relieve the suffering of many people from anxiety. Like "Nighthawks," this painting thus is highly meaningful, albeit gloomy.

ARTWORKS CAN EXPRESS BIG TRUTHS

Although the main meaning of artworks is to express emotion, they can also give us in vivid and powerful ways truths such as life-truths and truths about deep values, for examples, goodness and justice. These are extremely hard to know in our scientific age with its insistence on physical facts alone as proof. Artworks can make much meaning for us by giving us such big truths, as in the three following extended examples.

First, this partial poem "Harlem" by writer Langston Hughes exemplifies how an artwork can express big truths about our lives:

What happens to a dream deferred?
Does it dry up
like a raisin in the sun?

Does it stink like rotten meat?

Maybe it sags
like a heavy load.

Or does it just explode?

Hughes' poem tells us with forceful metaphors such as stinking, rotting meat and dreams exploding the big truth that if we postpone attaining our "dreams" or cherished aspirations too long, they become denied in effect. This is true for individuals as well as social groups such as blacks.

Hughes wrote in "Harlem" that a dream deferred "dries up like a raisin in the sun." This powerful metaphor became the title of Lorraine Hansberry's play protesting housing segregation. When this play became a hit on Broadway, it helped change the law in the Constitution of the United States that allowed it.

Hughes' poem "Harlem" also inspired activist Martin Luther King's assertion that "a dream deferred is a dream denied," This became a slogan in the Civil Rights Movement of the 1960's. Thus, Hughes' vivid metaphors in his poem "Harlem" helped Hansberry, the U. S. Supreme Court and M. L. King to know the life-truth that we need to act on our aspirations before it becomes too late to realize them.

THE CHICAGO PICASSO: THE MYSTERY OF CITIES

The Chicago Picasso

The second extended example of how artworks can express big truths comes from the untitled sculpture by Picasso in the Daley Plaza, Chicago, commonly called "The Chicago Picasso." Does this abstract sculpture show the front of a bird with its wings spread? Or does it depict a thin-faced woman with long hair? Or yet does it look like the face of a skinny Afghan hound?

Many other interpretations of Picasso's sculpture are possible and welcome. **Whatever this sculpture pictures, I can interpret the big truth that huge cities like Chicago are complex mysteries of diverse richness in, for examples, their residents' customs, clothing, culture, arts, cuisines and the like.** This might well be the reason that Picasso's sculpture has become a main symbol—today called an "icon" --for Chicago. Set in the Daley Plaza downtown, many Chicagoans and tourists can think on a daily basis about this sculpture. (Do you get the pun? Ha! Ha!)

LIFE-TRUTHS IN BEETHOVEN'S "SYMPHONY #9"

Ludwig Von Beethoven

My third extended example of how an artwork can express big truths is Ludwig Von Beethoven's "Ninth Symphony," even though it has no words to say them, like the Picasso sculpture. These truths come through interpreting these artworks, as summarized at the very start of this chapter.

The dark and stormy turmoil that starts this symphony can be interpreted as expressing Beethoven's mighty struggles with his gigantic losses. He had just lost while still young his "dearly beloved" (whoever she was—his copyist?) and his hearing. These are the biggest losses that can afflict a composer of music.

The Second Movement musicalizes Beethoven's bitterly disappointing experiences. Yet, it does so in a beautiful way suggesting the ability of his will power to transcend such

disappointments. He develops this fully in the Fourth Movement after making the highest stakes in the Third one.

The Third Movement starts as Beethoven begins to get an answer from his calls to God as to why he has lost so much meaning so soon in his life. However, this is interrupted by blaring fanfares from brass instruments that sound like hammer blows knocking at Heaven's door—shades of "fate [death] knocking at the door" heard in the famous four-note theme of da-da-da-dah in his outstanding "Fifth Symphony" and Bob Dylan's song "Knocking at Heaven's Door." **God does not answer Beethoven's plaintive calls. This movement ends with his calm acceptance of this very sad fact.**

The Fourth Movement most unusually opens with an outburst of dissonance (or notes that do not harmonize) to show that Beethoven defied even God. The music then turns to an ethereal tune of joy. Out of his own will power Beethoven expresses much happiness. He thus gives us the great gift of his genius forever.

At the end of the Fourth Movement, he set to lively music writer Friedrich Schiller's inspirational poem "Ode to Joy" testifying to the brotherhood of all people. The "Ninth Symphony" became the first choral symphony, even if only at its end.

Beethoven thus expresses the big truth that he (and us) can feel joy and brotherhood simply because of our sheer will to do so despite severe meaninglessness in our lives, like his total deafness, bitter heartbreak and God's failure to respond to his cries.

He just experienced another huge disappointment when Napoleon crowned himself emperor of Europe. Distraught, Beethoven ripped off his dedication of a recently composed piano concerto to him. Napoleon had espoused innovative democracy and laws, but he had clearly become a narcissistic egomaniac.

Again, Beethoven in his "Ninth Symphony" made much meaning despite his huge losses by expressing life-truths that one's will can overcome these and that we can find joy on our own without God with the help of geniuses in the arts and big truths such as Schiller's universal brotherhood. So you can learn such big truths by interpreting this symphony (and other artworks).

How can you make more meaning for yourself than by learning the big truths expressed in such works of artworks treated in this section (Hughes' "Harlem," the Chicago Picasso and Beethoven's "Ninth Symphony") and feeling the big but specific emotions expressed by them? I myself do not know any way.

ART CRITICISM AS MAKING MEANING

The highest level of the philosophy of art is art criticism in which you make a judgment about whether an artwork is good or bad. **The key to unlocking art criticism is to find a proper standard to judge artworks by.** This tells you what to consider in an artwork when judging it. A standard gives you a reason (or ground) to back up your specific judgments of an artwork.

The following lists the main critical standards for judging artworks that have been used throughout history:

realistic imitation, proper proportion or harmony and beauty— explained shortly below in "Beauty" (mostly from Plato and Aristotle);

big truths revealed (from the Enlightenment);

powerful emotions expressed (from the Romantics who strongly reacted against the Enlightenment);

organic or living whole in which no part can be removed from an artwork without lessening the life of the whole;

art for art's sake, not to imitate things, but to appreciate abstract artworks that create their own worlds of shapes, colors and sounds;

glorifying the lives of workers (from Marxism);

artworks that are **useful for living better daily lives** (from American pragmatism); and

many others because of the great diversity of standards implied in by the richness of artworks. Which is the best standard of art criticism from the many candidates? My answer should be obvious by now, but first I want to indicate an intriguing predecessor to it.

Johann Goethe

Writer Johann Goethe concisely wrote that any person criticizing or judging an artwork ought to ask three questions: 1. what is the artist trying to do? 2. does she succeed in doing it? and 3. is it worth doing? His questions imply that making meaning or having impact is the needed standard for art criticism. While Goethe offered rich insights into art criticism, he did not make making meaning explicit as the long-needed standard for judging artworks.

What better standard can there be than that a good artwork makes meaning or has an (mostly emotional) impact on its audience? Much of this impact is positive, of course, but not for such artworks as "Nighthawks" and "The Scream" just treated. These impacts can also be on our thinking, as also has just been treated. Those artworks that express emotional meaning most directly ought to be judged best.

So, **the best question to ask regarding the criticism of an artwork is how deeply does it have an emotional impact on most of its audience?** The criticism of an artwork ought to describe or explain its special features that produce its emotions in its audience.

AN EXCELLENT WORK: MICHELANGELO'S "DAVID"

Michelangelo, "David"

An extended example of art criticism as making emotional meaning can come from Michelangelo's sculpture **"David." This artwork has for five centuries had much positive emotional impact on its millions of viewers for many of its features. One of the first features is that it has the ideal male form in his musculature**. Another such feature is that David has the calm look of supreme confidence that with God's help he will slay with only his slingshot the enemy giant Goliath who has a sword.

Other emotion-evoking features in this sculpture include how boy-like David is nude to show not only that he is vulnerable to being embarrassed, but also that he has much dignity. He has large hands to do his heroic task. The appearance on his face carefully calculates his combat with Goliath. David's neck is tense, his veins bulge and his brow is drawn. His twisting body conveys that his thinking puts him in muscular motion, as does Rodin's sculpture "The Thinker." (See the start of Chapter 1.) "David" certainly has many features that evoke emotions.

All of these features are so meaningful on our emotions that "David" has come to show male beauty to the world for five centuries. The colossal size of this marble sculpture alone is monumental. It is as if Michelangelo somehow brought David back to life. Therefore, for all these features that produce emotions in their viewers, **we can criticize or judge this sculpture as an excellent artwork.**

A GOOD ARTWORK: RAVEL'S BOLERO"

dance, "Bolero"

Another—but lesser--extended example of art criticism as making meaning is composer Maurice Ravel's "Bolero" because of its powerful emotional impact on listeners. He took this piece from a lively Spanish dance that features sharp turns with one hand over the dancer's head. The music of **"Bolero" becomes louder, but not faster as most listeners believe. Its simple repetitive dance theme becomes mesmerizing in its intensity, as it steams to its finale. This theme sounds as if something marvelous is about to happen. However, the very end sounds much like a discordant fizzle or "daaaaa."** This could remind listeners of times when they thought that events in their lives would make much meaning, but did not, as happens in the movie "Ten." **Or it might suggest that our entire lives lack meaning in the end.** Oh! Woe is us!

According to art criticism as making meaning, the stirring emotion of anticipating something marvelous about to happen expressed in "Bolero" has so much impact on the emotions of its listeners that it ought to be judged a good artwork, but not a great one because it expresses only one emotion repeatedly louder.

Bad artworks do not make much emotional meaning or impact on their audiences. We can judge artworks that show weak emotions or trivial ones as bad, for examples, almost all modern sculptures. Also, a movie or a play that appeals to its audience's prurient interests or morbid curiosity is not a good artwork according to the standard of making meaning, no matter how successful it is financially--which it is likely to be! Alas!

People often implicitly use this standard of making meaning, as did Goethe at the start of this section. Yet, it helps much to make it explicit to use it expeditiously. We much need such a standard stated strongly to settle vast confusion and disagreements regarding judging artworks.

MAKING MEANING IN VAN GOGH'S NIGHT SKY

Van Gogh, "The Starry Night"

Another extended example of an artwork judged by the standard of making meaning as excellent is Vincent Van Gogh's painting "The Starry Night." Many artists, like him, search intensely for meaning their entire adult lives. After being expelled from the ministry because of his radical ideas and his unkempt looks, **he finally found much meaning in the night sky alive with the presence of God** in the insane asylum to which he had committed himself. **In this sky he saw such spiritual sights as interlocking shooting stars, a bright crescent moon, a cypress tree looking like a flame reaching into Heaven and brightly glowing stars above a sleeping village below with one light on—showing hope for us?** The painting's bright yellows in the glowing stars symbolize Jesus, to him.

Thus, in this painting **Van Gogh threw himself fully into the search for meaning. He thereby saw a night sky far more meaningful and spiritual than anyone has ever seen.** Do you now understand the outstanding effects of intensely seeking meaning in artworks? His "Starry Night" surely should be judged as an excellent artwork on the basis of such a standard.

BEAUTY

The highest value in the philosophy of art is beauty. In Plato's dialogue "The Symposium" the participants took turns defining it. This turns into a drunken orgy at the end! The character Socrates **defined "beauty" as "the everlasting possession of the good."** By this he **regarded beauty as a higher value than even the good because it captures images of the good and holds them for us to experience forever**, for examples, a hero represented in a sculpture, poem or painting.

The Parthenon Temple

According to Plato, beauty is mostly mathematical, particularly geometrical consisting of circles, squares, triangles and the like. He considered these shapes perfect, for example, in a circle every point on the line is equidistant from its center.

The geometrical shapes in beautiful artworks have the proper proportions, ratios or harmonies for them. For example, the majestic Parthenon Temple in ancient Athens (and many Greek and

Roman temples around the Mediterranean Sea) has the proportions of one in its height, three across its front and nine in its length along its sides. With such exquisite proportions, it is no wonder that the Parthenon still looks beautiful to millions of tourists after twenty-five centuries!

As is typical throughout Plato's dialogues, the proper proportions, ratios, or harmonies of an artwork often remain mysterious. However, we can find these often embodied, for examples, in the superb sounds of symphonies and in the ideal meters and rhythms of poems. If artists did know all the perfect proportions, they would be able to create beautiful artworks.

Beauty is widely thought to be highly subjective, as evidenced in the popular saying, "Beauty is in the eye of the beholder." However, Plato's argument that beautiful artworks have **proper proportions gives beauty a degree of objectivity because these must be physically embodied in artworks in their shapes that we can observe.** However, again, we need not despise subjectivity. We can never escape it entirely. In fact, it is often our most meaningful task that we need to know more about. We also need to be objective to survive, just as do other animals. However, they cannot prosper or flourish by creating beauty as humans can. **Beauty is our greatest glory.**

Plato wrote in his dialogue "Ion" that **beautiful artworks have metaphorical "wings to soar" above our highly imperfect world**.

Beauty in artworks therefore can be an extremely rich source of making meaning because it has total freedom to express grand emotions and truths. We much need this in our age of gross materialism when greed is commonly thought to be good (as asserted in the movie "Wall Street"), indeed, the greatest good. We should be very grateful for beautiful artworks, particularly the traditional ones, for their vivid displays of meaningful emotions. These artworks show tremendous achievements in realism, as in traditional paintings of humans in their environments, for example, Da Vinci's "Last Supper." Abstract art has now run its course, being over one hundred years old and no longer having shocking or revolutionary meaning for us, although its possibilities are endless.

John Keats

Beautiful artworks enable us to transcend even the abundant meaninglessness of the Earth into the timeless realm of beauty where we can eternally experience them. As poet John Keats famously wrote, "A thing of beauty is a joy forever;" for example, Michelangelo's sculpture "Pieta" in which sorrowful youthful- looking Mary holds the limp crucified Christ in her soft lap made from hard marble can everlastingly give us joy because of its beauty.

Beauty can transform negative experiences, including even death, into something of lasting value, as in some poems such as "Death, Be Not Proud" by John Donne and several by Lord Bryon. These poems encourage readers with the hope of the after-life through their souls which was more real faith in their times.

It would be hard to make more meaning for oneself in any other field of philosophy than art because **you can avail yourself at any**

time to your cell-phone to, for example, help quickly interpret an artwork. There you have the whole world of knowing—but also buying and selling, boo!--at your fingertips to help you richly experience a work of art.

It also would be hard to make more meaning for others in any other field of philosophy than by a talented artist who knows how to make meaning in her artworks, but this goes beyond the present chapter.

We all want to make meaning unknowingly at least. Can we ever make enough of it? No! **We want only to love beautiful artworks,** not to primarily possess them, claimed Aquinas. All of us feel very good when we make meaning from artworks. We can readily achieve this if we make a little effort to use the many ideas and topics in this chapter: experiencing artworks (especially interpreting them), sheerly sensing them, regarding the grand emotions and new truths expressed by them, judging them as good or bad by the meaning that they make and appreciating beauty as proper proportions.

EXERCISES:

1. Describe your experience of an artwork. You can use a classic painting or piece of classical music on-line.

2. Interpret an artwork by using some fruitful knowledge about it and your imagination on it.

3. Describe one artwork which you find fascinating for you just to experience or sense.

4. Interpret an artwork in terms of the emotions that it expresses to you.

5. Criticize an artwork as good or bad in terms of the emotional meaning that it makes on you.

6. Explain why you consider an artwork beautiful. Do you agree with Plato's views on beauty?

Chapter 9

MAKING MEANING BY THE PHILOSOPHY OF GOD

$$X$$

x

God exists.   *No God exists.*

X = you

If the God of Christianity truly exists, He would have maximum meaning because He could grant each person everlasting joy in Heaven or literal Hellfire. The diagram above shows the importance of the question of whether or not God truly exists, called "the God-question." **No other field of philosophy offers to make so much meaning in terms of joy in Heaven and time—immortality—for you, yet has such excruciating little evidence to support it.**

Determining the meaning of God can be compared to two explorers on a journey through their lives. One explorer fervently believes that her journey will end with her eternal joy in Heaven with her loved ones. The other explorer firmly maintains that there will be absolutely nothing at the end of her journey, not even awareness of blackness.

Which explorer is correct? How do we know the truth in this? **To know the meaning of God, we must rely on the philosophy of knowledge of rationalism** because it goes beyond Plato's cave of the senses. (See Chapter 5 on "Rationalism.")

Late in his life Shakespeare agreed with the sentiment expressed by the second explorer in the following lines from Macbeth:

> Life's but a walking shadow, a poor player
> That struts and frets his hour upon the stage
> And then is heard no more, it is a tale
> Told by an idiot, full of sound and fury
> Signifying nothing.

The Hubble Telescope recently showed us that **there are trillions of galaxies, each with trillions of stars with planets**. These are expanding. Into what? The best answer now is into mathematical systems and unknown types of space. But then what is beyond these? This is most mind-blowing! However, the relevant question now regarding your making immortal meaning is, **"Would God even care about the inhabitants of the tiny planet Earth among trillions of others?"** This seems quite hard even for God.

Let's define "God" as "the supernatural creator of the universe who cares about humans." God must be more than the universe or be "supernatural" to create it from nothing. The traditional definition of God also conceives of Him as caring about humans to grant them immortal after-lives. This definition is crucial to knowing whether or not God and hence our joyful immortal meaning exists.

We cannot discuss in this chapter God's possible traits such as being all-powerful, all-knowing and all-good because that would be much too long and debatable.

Thinking people seek much to know the answer to the God-question to find out whether or not the maximum meaning of the after-life is true. We must be as reasonable as we can on this question, but it is hard to even know when we are being so.

The most reasonable way to know whether or not God exists is by the "arguments" (in its special sense of "arguing for," not "disagreements") for God's existence and their criticisms. (See Chapter 4 on "Think in Terms of Arguments.") Like all logical arguments, these consist of premises that give evidence for or reasons to believe that the conclusion, in the present case that "God exists," is true.

The three logically soundest (or strongest) arguments for the existence of God are 1) the creator or first cause of the universe argument, 2) the divine designer or planner of the Earth argument and

3) the personal experiences of God argument. Let's examine each of these in turn for their soundness. By doing so, we will mine the rich veins of thinking about God's possible existence and thus our maximum meaning of being immortal.

THE CREATOR OR FIRST CAUSE ARGUMENT FOR GOD

Diagram of the Creator or Cosmological
Argument for God's Existence

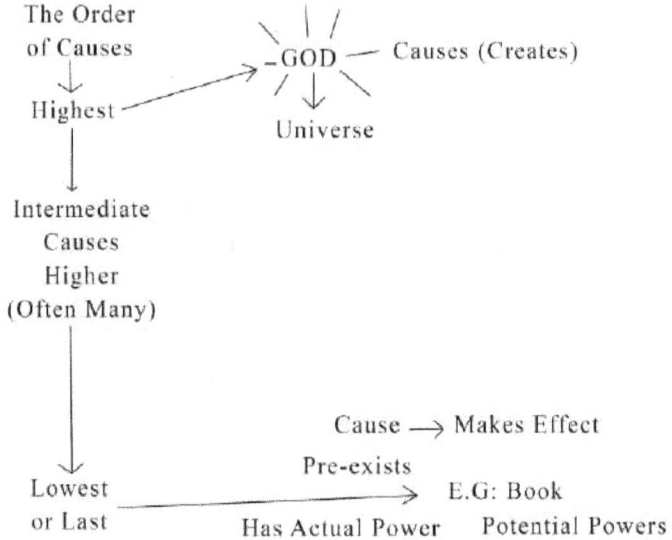

The Order
of Causes

Highest

Intermediate
Causes
Higher
(Often Many)

Lowest
or Last

GOD — Causes (Creates)

Universe

Cause → Makes Effect
Pre-exists
→ E.G: Book
Has Actual Power   Potential Powers

Diagram of the Creator Argument for God

This argument is based on the universal law that everything needs a cause to make it exist. A cause obviously must pre-exist or be prior in time to its effect to make it. Thus, there must be a prior cause that makes the universe exist, according to the creator argument.

Parmenides, one of the first philosophers, wrote that, "Nothing comes from nothing." Plato then posited the view that the universe or what he called **"the cosmos"** had to be caused to move by a self-moving mover. **Aristotle held the even more puzzling view that**

there are "unmoved movers." To him, these unchangeable entities "think about thinking." He believed that there must be a cause to explain why the universe exists, but he did not develop this much. These ancient views helped to slowly develop the creator or first because argument expressed first, but briefly, by Aquinas around 1270 A. D.

The creator argument assumes the premise that the universe could conceivably not exist, so its existence requires a cause or reason in order for it (or anything) to exist. Furthermore, **if the universe did not have a cause, there would be a time—at its very beginning— at which nothing exists. Nothing could exist later from nothing. Yet things obviously exist now. So, it is necessary that the universe was caused by something other than itself or, in other words, by God.**

Another strong premise of the creator argument is that causes have actual powers whereas effects have only potential ones. For example (from Aquinas), fire has the actual power of heat. So, it can give it to a piece of wood which has the potential to be hot. **Similarly, a cause like God has the actual power to make potentialities like the universe exist**, according to this premise.

Yet another strong premise—the strongest one--of the causal argument for a creator of the universe rests in the order of causes. (See the left side of the diagram for the creator argument.) **An order is made by a cause being higher than its effects** since it pre-exists and makes them exist.

The order of causes begins with the last effect, for example, this book. **Next in this order are higher intermediate causes** which occur between the last and the highest causes. There are often many of these, for examples, those causes involved in writing and making this book. **In the order of causes, intermediate causes are higher than the last**

effect because they pre-exist it and make it exist. These cause everything in nature or the universe to happen.

The proof itself of God's existence resides in the highest or first cause needing to be higher than all the intermediate causes which cause all the effects in nature, as just explained. So, there must be in the order of causes a first cause higher than even the nature or the universe itself. This first cause is thereby supernatural or higher than all of nature because it caused the universe to exist according to the order of causes.

Being the supernatural creator or higher than all of nature or the universe defines "God" in large part except for caring about humans which is the topic of the second argument for God's existence. (See this definition of "God" at the start of this chapter.) Aquinas wrote about the first cause higher than all of nature itself that, "We call this God."

Causes cannot regress to infinity because **even such an endless regress had to begin somewhere.** Can the universe always exist of itself as a brute given fact? No, because if it did it would have no cause for it to exist as such a fact. **Everything that exists needs a cause that made it exist.** The universe is not totally irrational as its brute or eternal existence would require. It has many rational aspects such as its scientific laws that govern it, for example, gravity.

THE BIG BANG

An advanced scientific finding that strongly supports the creator argument goes by the striking, but incorrect, name "the Big Bang." This charts the very beginning of the universe. **The Bang was an explosion of an unknown infinitesimal point or what is called a "singularity" which contained all the universe's energy and space-time into a huge ball of matter and space** that keeps inflating or expanding from its center into emptiness. It had an unimaginably high density and temperature. The Big Bang initiated space itself. There is no evidence of any phenomena prior to it.

Scientists (actually astronomers and cosmologists) have determined that the **Big Bang took place approximately 13.8 billion years ago. This is the age of the universe. There was no time before the Big Bang because there was no universe or matter for it then. Time requires an eternal God to create or cause it.**

We do not know now if there was any matter or space before the Big Bang. However, that seems quite impossible because both of these require a cause to exist. Like time, matter and space require an eternal God to cause them to exist. Thus, **the advanced scientific findings of** the Big Bang strongly sup- ports the first cause argument for a creator (God) of the universe.

THE DESIGN ARGUMENT FOR GOD

DIAGRAM OF DESIGN ARGUMENT FOR GOD'S EXISTENCE
- FROM AQUINAS & PALEY

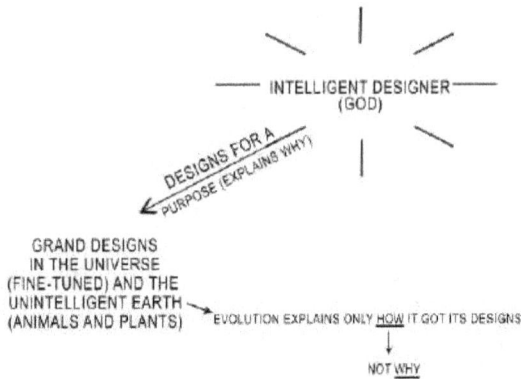

INTELLIGENT DESIGNER
(GOD)

DESIGNS FOR A PURPOSE (EXPLAINS WHY)

GRAND DESIGNS
IN THE UNIVERSE
(FINE-TUNED) AND THE
UNINTELLIGENT EARTH
(ANIMALS AND PLANTS)   EVOLUTION EXPLAINS ONLY HOW IT GOT ITS DESIGNS

NOT WHY

The second logically sound argument for the existence of God rests on the complex and grand design (plan) that exists mostly in plants and animals on Earth. This design could not happen by chance, but must be designed by God because of its grand complexity, according to this argument. There are innumerable examples of this: the wonderful beauty of flowers, the countless species of amazing animals adapted to all extremes of environment, intricate genes, instincts in animals (such as the migration of large flocks of birds), a sunny summer day, every snowflake being different and the marvelous bodies of animals such as the complexity of their eyes, which has been used as the main example by philosophers since 1857—more on this shortly below.

Don't these grand examples require God to divinely design them, not to create them as in the creator or first cause argument? **An**

intelligent planner (God) is required to produce the patterns of survival and even beauty from the many possibilities. The more that scientists, for example, Einstein quoted above and biologist Charles Darwin quoted below, study these designs the more that they are impressed by them.

We can conceive of the Divine Designer also as a supreme architect, craftsman and engineer. (These terms belong in the upper-right of the diagram for the design argument.)

The designs on Earth favor humans. If they were slightly off, we would not have developed on this planet. The Divine Designer deliberately used the laws that would allow humans to flourish on Earth, according to the argument from design. So, such intelligent designs as humans demand an Intelligent Designer or God.

The argument from design's logical soundness fundamentally depends on whether or not the designs of the Earth justify your feelings of awe, defined as "a feeling of reverence," when you contemplate the wonders of the world. If you are justified in feeling much of this, then the design argument is sound. Are the designs of the Earth awesome or not? The answer is rather obvious.

HISTORY OF DESIGN ARGUMENT

The design argument is the oldest in western philosophy. Thinkers who lived even before Socrates were impressed by the enormous orderliness of the Earth, often with special reference to the regular revolving of the stars, the sun and the moon. So even ancient thinkers agreed that intelligent design rules the world.

Plato cleverly presented the grand design of the Earth as a "likely story" in the form of a myth. His supremely intelligent god grandly designed the Earth out of its pre-existing chaotic matter. This deity also designed the universe, for example, the stars, to weakly imitate perfect ideas of them. (See "Plato's Allegory of the Cave" in Chapter 2.)

Aristotle understood all living things in the natural world as striving to actualize their potentials. He thought that this most completely explains them. He regarded all things in nature as having a purpose to fulfill; for examples, for birds to fly and for humans to think—a philosopher like him would need to favor that last example! Ha! Ha!

Charles Darwin

Like Plato, Aristotle thought that an Intelligent Planner guides all nature. The ideas on design of both philosophers, especially Aristotle's emphasis on the complexity of biology, remained influential until Darwin's theory of evolution exposed even more of this complexity according to scientific laws. He had meticulously shown how this complexity, especially for numerous species of animals, resulted from the struggle for survival of the fittest which he called "natural selection." This is done by the genes in the DNA, but this is too technical to treat here.

Evolution came to be regarded as the instrument that God used to design the world. However, it does offer a completely

scientific explanation of it. **This dispenses with the need of a designing God. Also, it is simpler** than the view that God used evolution. Science instructs us to prefer the simpler hypothesis. Evolution is simpler so it seems preferable.

However, **Darwin's theory of evolution explains only how animals and plants got the grand design that they have, not why they did. The argument from design explains this why: God created such designs to give beauty to many organisms and prosperity to humans.**

William Paley

Philosophers favoring the design argument tried to further strengthen it in the face of evolution's frontal attacks on it. These philosophers then developed other aspects of the argument, especially comparing the complex plan of the Earth to a watch.

In the eighteenth century, philosopher William Paley wrote that in "crossing a heath suppose I pitched my foot" against a watch. (He was referring to a pocket watch that was popular at that time. (If he lived today, he probably would have kicked a beloved cell-phone that someone had lost. Ha! Ha!)

Paley concluded that the watch was complexly constructed by a designer, very probably a human for the specific purpose of telling time. Remove or rearrange any of its intricate workings and the watch no longer has a purpose. From these reasonings Paley inferred that the watch must have a designer who planned it for the purpose to tell time.

Likewise, the Earth must have a Divine Designer who planned it to have the purpose of evolving intelligent life in the form of humans. Thus, it or an Intelligent Planner exists according to the analogy of the watch. Again, such amazing complexity of the Earth can be explained only by the existence of a Divine Designer who plans and directs it toward its goals of prosperity and beauty.

Yet, the watch is only an analogy or comparison. This is the weakest type of argument in logic, but it is one.

Scientists have now determined that life in the universe would not be possible if two dozen properties of it were even slightly different from what they are. For example, if the force binding neutrons to protons had differed by five per cent, life would not be possible. **This fact is called the "fine tuning" of the Earth for life.** The only two ways to explain fine tuning are either chance or a Divine Designer. Would many rational or logical people accept the explanation that the amazing design of life on Earth exists because of blind chance? Hardly. Since the universe began at the Big Bang 13.75 billion years ago, the designs on Earth do not have endless time to evolve. However, they do have a looong time to evolve. (See the preceding section of this chapter on the Big Bang.)

THE ARGUMENT FROM PERSONAL EXPERIENCES OF GOD

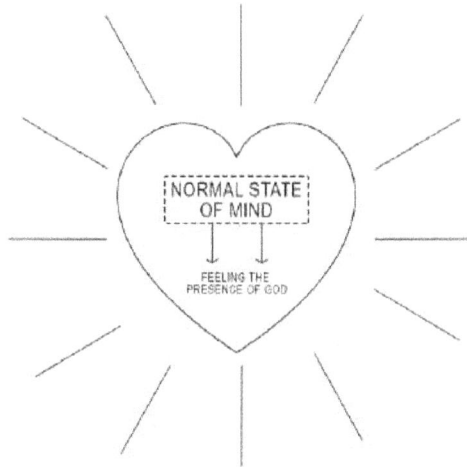

NORMAL STATE
OF MIND

FEELING THE
PRESENCE OF GOD

PERSONAL EXPERIENCE OF GOD

This third logically sound argument for the existence of God differs considerably from the previous two (creator or first cause and design) because it does not rely on abstract ideas, but **it relies instead the actual facts about God having revealed Himself as a living presence to humans. Many people claim that they "feel" and experience that God is somehow with them. This clearly proves that God exists.** (Philosophers call this the "mystical" argument, but it has nothing to do with mysteries.)

A personal experience of God can range from a simple one that God is with you, for examples, in nature or a church to an overwhelming union with God.

For an extended example of last type, mathematician and philosopher Blaise Pascal wrote on a note pinned to his undershirt for the rest of his life about the experience that he had with God on November 23, 1654: "Joy, joy, joy! Eternal joy! From about 10:30 last night until 12:30 FIRE! God of Abraham . . . Certitude, certitude, feeling, joy, peace!"

(This is the longest personal experience of God recorded in the West, as most are flashes of a union with the divine. Buddha In the mystical East is said to have experienced a very different god for seven days and nights of bliss.)

People who, like Pascal, experienced God personally attest that this is ineffable or cannot adequately be expressed in words. Such experiences are much more like feelings than ideas. **A person who experiences God feels joy or, like Pascal, even a "totally blown out high!"** as hippies expressed this in the 1960's. Nevertheless, such an experience does give one intellectual truth, namely, that "God exists."

People who experience God such as Pascal are convinced that the divine exists. **They do not need to reason or argue this, for they have experienced God. In other words, they do not find the divine in their heads, but rather in their hearts.** (See diagram of "Personal Experiences of God" at the start of this chapter.) They find God inside themselves rather than outside. For people who have personally experienced God, the unseen reality of God is far more meaningful than anything that they sense imprisoned in Plato's cave. They have felt the divine living presence.

Aquinas wrote that his many detailed books on theology and philosophy, including his famous five arguments for God's existence, were "like so much straw" after he had a profound personal experience of God. He never wrote another line. His long quest for God was ended.

EXAMPLES OF PERSONAL EXPERI-ENCES OF GOD

MOSES

An extended example of a person who experienced God is the revered prophet in several religions (Judaism, Christianity and Islam), Moses. According to the Biblical book "Exodus," he repeatedly talked to God and performed miracles with divine help. It is written that Moses even saw God, but only His backside. Unfortunately for others, he did not describe what this looks like except that He descended as a bright cloud. God told him that, "You cannot see my face because no one shall see me." The allusion in this passage to God's face builds on the Judeo-Christian belief in the Biblical book "Genesis" that humans were "made in God's image" and so are able to experience God.

PAUL OF TARSUS

Saul, his Hebrew name, persecuted the first Christians until God unseated him from his horse on the road to Damascus and asked him why he was doing so. **Paul was so overwhelmed by his experience of God that he became the primary missionary and theologian for the new religion of Christianity,** even though he never heard or talked to Jesus.

THERESA OF AVILA

Bernini, "The Ecstasy of Saint Theresa"

Yet still another extended example of a person who claimed to experience God many times, Theresa of Avila, shows that the intensity of an experience of God does not guarantee that it is a genuine encounter. Theresa was a nun and thus celibate, that is, she never had sex. She described one of her ecstatic experiences of God in the following way: "I know that my Divine Spouse [God] is near. I cannot help complaining to Him in words of love. I am consumed by desire. My soul feels a spark stronger than ever to endure the love- pain that she has just experienced."

Theresa is in this quote satisfying or "sublimating," as Freud would have gleefully expressed the matter, her sex-drive by imagining that she is having sex with God. In the sculpture by Bernini above, she looks as if she is having an orgasm! Her experience of God was clearly a delusion or mistaken perception that arose from her subconsciousness, which is ninety per cent of the brain's activity.

Although Theresa's experience of God is very vulnerable to the criticisms just made of it, **there needs to only one genuine case of a experience of God for it to be a strong argument for God's existence.** For example, is Moses nothing but a terrific story? Also, was Pascal in a delusional state of mind when he experienced God? That event totally changed his life, as it did for Paul and many others who claimed that they experienced God.

It might be objected that there are no examples of people who experienced God in recent times, but there are at least two such examples of highly unlikely people who have strong claims that they experienced Mary, the revered mother of Jesus for Catholics.

Marian Grotto at Lourdes, France

The first of these experiences occurred in 1858 in Lourdes, France, where Mary appeared eighteen times in a grotto to a miller's daughter named Bernadette. This peasant girl was later canonized or sainted after highly rigorous tests by the Catholic Church determined that these apparitions were genuine.

The second apparition of Mary happened in 1917 to three shepherd children in Fatima, Portugal. There Mary appeared six times visible only to them "brighter than the sun." A crowd of 70,000 people at one apparition saw what came to be called "the miracle of the sun." Most of the crowd saw a multi-colored disk dance in the sky and zigzag back toward the Earth. However, thousands of people present reported not seeing anything unusual. The Catholic Church shortly thereafter declared the three children's visions of Mary, including one of Hell at her first apparition to them, "worthy of belief." They were canonized as saints in 2017 on the centennial of the Marian apparitions to them.

Does all this show that argument from personal experiences of God is sound? There appears to be much evidence, especially genuine examples, for this, particularly Pascal, Moses, Paul, Bernadette of Lourdes and the three children of Fatima who would have no reason for deceiving others.

THE PROBLEM OF EVIL

Atheists deny the existence of any God. They loudly protest—and correctly--that most people tend to believe in God only so that they think that they will not have to really die. (See section on Freud below in this chapter.) So the question of human immortal meaning is again raised by atheism, especially by its main problem of evil which will be treated now.

The problem of evil is commonly called "the atheist's problem." **This problem is defined as "why is there so much evil if an all- good or even good God exists?"** This is the biggest problem in all philosophy, even bigger than the existence of God. Evils are not just "the absence of good," as philosopher Augustine wrote. They are quite real and hard to explain in view of God's goodness. We need to solve the problem of evil if we are to make immortal meaning by God, the atheist asserts.

"Evil" is defined as "any undeserved pain or suffering." Perhaps the most horrendous example of evil is found in writer Fyodor Dostoyevsky's lengthy novel "The Brothers Karamazov" which searches for God. In one scene he described how **invading soldiers make a captured mother's baby smile and then shoot the infant in the head in front of her.**

There is so much evil that it is hard to give more examples, but here are some major ones: friends and even lovers betraying each other; severe birth defects and mental retardation in newborns; Alzheimer's disease and others such as pandemics; racial and other forms of unwarranted hatred; many unjust wars in which literally millions of young men and civilians have been murdered and even slaughtered--see Chapter 6 on "Intangibles We Live For"--; and the inexorable death of all living things which is the ultimate evil for them.

THE STORY OF JOB

The classic Christian solution of the problem of evil and God comes from the Biblical book of "Job." He is described as a "righteous man, blessed with wealth, sons and daughters." Satan claims that Job would surely "curse God" if all his wealth, children and servants were taken away. God then permits Satan to do this as a test of Job's love. At first Job praises God: "The Lord gives and the Lord takes away. Blessed be the name of the Lord." (The book of "Job" is highly poetic.)

Later because of his suffering Job laments that he was born and he longs to die. Even that is forbidden to him. Then he demands that God answer his cries. God does so, but only to assert His authority, asking Job, "Where were you when I laid the foundations of the Earth?" Job then concedes by making a "burnt offering." God then finally restored all his wealth and children. He lived to see to the fourth generation of them.

The story of Job thus does not offer us any logical or rational solution to the problem of evil. This Biblical account tells us only to have blind or unquestioning faith in the power of God to make and take away evil whenever He desires to do so if a person submits by praying.

Anyone who wants to believe in an all-good or even good God— what other kind is there?--needs to first develop her own theodicy defined as "a defense or justification of God's goodness to vindicate how much evil exists alongside it." Would a good God permit so much evil as the smiling baby murdered in front of her mother? A theodicy answers this question why God permits so much evil to happen while preserving divine goodness to solve the problem of evil to restore a good God who can grant us immortal meaning.

TYPES OF EVIL

To develop a theodicy, we first need to distinguish two main types of evil. The first is natural evil defined as "evil which the world inflicts on us." Examples of this type include earthquakes, epidemics from viruses—although COVID-19 was made by humans, as has been noted--, cancers, floods and forest fires. In the last example quite cute fawns and other innocent animals are burned alive in agony. **These natural phenomena inflict evils on innocent victims without a perpetrator to blame and no accompanying mitigating good.**

The main theodicy for natural evil is that God's laws must hold for evil as well as good. God must apply these laws everywhere; for examples, fires can warm us but they also can burn us, and knives can cut our food but they also can cut our flesh. **However, as Plato concluded long ago, this theodicy makes laws superior to God.** Is God even less than these laws? Hardly! So the soundest theodicy for natural evil fails.

The second type of evil is moral, defined as "evils that humans inflict on others." This type of evil is frequent. Some more common examples include lying, cheating, stealing, raping, hating and murdering. According to Christian theology, moral evil results whenever a person defies a divine law.

The soundest theodicy for moral evils is that they result from human free will to choose them. A person's free choice is responsible for moral evil. We make meaning of God's goodness if we regard God as creating humans to be free rather than mere automata or robots like the rest of nature, according to this view. It has recently received much development, especially by theologian John Hick.

HICK'S THEODICY OF SOUL-MAKING

According to Hick, humans are still in the process of evolving from the image of God into His likeness. He maintains that this is developed out of choosing good over evil.

Hick acknowledges that some evil serves no constructive purpose and can even destroy an individual. He replies to this that, **nevertheless, without free will humans could not develop highly valuable feelings of sympathy and compassion. We need these feelings to develop genuine love for others and God**. For this reason, a loving God, according to Hick's theodicy, would create humans with free will despite the enormous evil that they can choose to inflict. A world without evil and suffering could not be a place where humans can develop morally. **To Hick, God gave humans the great gift of free will as a test of a person's love of Him by learning to choose good over evil.** He did not create humans for our pleasure or for Earth to be a paradise for us, but to be a place where we can learn how to love God and others so that we can make our souls worthy of making meaning immortally, Hick maintains, although he does not use these terms.

Critics complain in Hick's theodicy that the test of free will is too hard at times as, for examples, Job before he made a burnt offering and the mother whose laughing baby was murdered in front of her. **Shouldn't a loving father give his clueless children more guidance about such horrible evils? Jesus said nothing about the problem of evil** which is the biggest one for atheists, as I have written.

Jesus himself sometimes mentioned "burning in the eternal fires of Hell." There cannot be a harsher or more severe punishment for making supposedly free choices. Hick does not analyze the extremely complex idea of free will. If he did so, he would learn how incredibly hard it is to make free choices. (See Chapter 12 on free will.)

Further, according to Christian scriptures, God expelled Adam and Eve from the Garden of Eden, and hence immortality because they ate an apple from the Tree of Knowledge. This contradicts Hicks' theodicy because it severely punishes humans for making free choices. (Again, see Chapter 12 on free will.)

A final theodicy is to limit God's goodness or power (or both) to control evil. Praying to an all-good God will not lessen the horrible effects of the current pandemic of the Corona Virus, for example. **Praying to God to grant favors bribes him in effect.** This theodicy regards a limited God as still evolving in His ability to control the tremendous amount of daily evil and meaninglessness. The **limited-God theodicy does explain why there is so much evil because God cannot conquer the huge amount of it.**

This theodicy is not likely to be popular as it is not based on the traditional concepts of God as all-good and almighty. Nevertheless, it is sound according to the laws of logic. (See Chapter 4.)

Thus, it is quite hard to make much meaning by solving the problem of evil versus God's goodness. This is to be expected whenever there are such extremely high stakes as God and immortal joy or endless Hellfire.

FREUD'S CRITICISM OF THE CHRISTIAN GOD: MANY BELIEVE DUE TO FEARING DEATH

Famous psychologist Sigmund **Freud severely criticized the widespread belief in the Christian concept of God as a loving father. He criticized this belief as juvenile because it is not mature enough to accept the factual reality of our deaths as the final end of our lives. He accused Christians of believing in a made-up father-figure beyond the sky who makes everything right in the end** by granting immortal happiness with one's loved ones.

Freud classified Christians in terms of their mental health as neurotics because they were too mentally weak and immature to accept the final reality of their physical deaths. In short, **he stressed that the fear of death causes people to believe in the Christian God.** Particularly as they become older, people tend to become more afraid that their deaths will result in nothingness and obliteration. They desperately seek salvation in a savior God, but **they are thinking irrationally out of fearing their deaths, according to Freud. To him, God is a massive delusion (or belief contradicted by reality) to Christians.**

Freud was right in criticizing the abuse of the Christian God and the improper use of Him as a crutch to enable people to walk through the meaningless of their lives in the—vain? See Chapter 11 on "Immortality" and "Resurrection" --belief that they would not remain dead. **However, he did not address the proper use of God, namely, to know whether or not He truly exists and thus whether or not we will live immortally.** Yet still again, no issues have more meaning than these because they have biggest amount of reality (God or not) and time (immortality or not) at stake.

AGNOSTICS

Agnostics hold that humans do not have the ability to know whether or not God really exists. They question that they can know whether or not God exists. (See Chapter 5 on knowing.) Agnostics claim that they cannot overcome their skeptical doubts about God's existence. They insist that the answer to the God-question is unknowable. Agnostics live, in effect, as atheists who do not believe that God exists.

Like atheists, agnostics demand physical or scientific evidence for all their beliefs, including God's existence. This does not violate their philosophy of knowing because the implied empirical philosophy of knowing of agnostics can know only physical facts. (See Chapter 5 on "Empiricism.")

Yet, **isn't it wiser if each person decides and acts about God's existence on the basis of the predominant knowledge that she has on this most meaningful issue?** Indeed! **We cannot wait until our deaths to find out the correct answer to the God-question because then it would be too late to show sincere concern.**

A main part of human dignity consists in critically and creatively continually thinking about the God-question during our entire adult lives. For the last time, what can make more meaning for yourself than knowing whether or not God exists and you will be immortal in Heaven? **Because you could make so much meaning by God you are not likely to do so.** The stakes are simply too huge and hard. **Nevertheless, you must try very hard, daily as I do by reading on the God-question, because that is the best way to get rational and logically-sound knowing about this most meaningful problem of God's existence.**

Amen! Amen!

Be it so! Be it so!

EXERCISES:

1. Explain one cause and its effect. How can the order of causes show that God exists?

2. Describe fully one design or seemingly divine plan for a plant or animal.

3. Discuss fully one personal experience of God, including possibly your own, that might be genuine.

4. You think that the arguments from the creator, design or personal experience show that God truly exists?

5. Describe one example of a horrible moral evil.

6. Explain fully your theodicy for solving the problem of so much evil and the existence of a good God.

7. Why is the God-question so meaningful overall to you?

Chapter 10

MAKING MEANING BY THE SELF

The question whether or not you will live immortally is intricately linked to issues surrounding what "the self" refers to, especially the soul which is taken to be immortal, but this question will be treated later in this chapter. Philosophers call this field not "the soul," but "the self."

Being in touch with your self can make much meaning for you, but this will also be treated later in this chapter.

The self is an individual person as the object of her own thinking, not her sensing. This is a highly subjective problem or field of philosophy and our lives. The self has much meaning for us because we are always in it. It is essentially the intangible source of an individual's consciousness and inner powers such as willing, feeling and desiring.

This philosophy of the self-expresses the first person or I, not the third or he or she (singular) or they (plural) and certainly not the second person or you.

All selves are unique because each has her own differing experiences through her life. So, each self has her own identity.

Since the self does not allow direct access to others, it is private. This privacy is one of many problems involved in knowing the self. These problems might be partially solved by empirical information regarding the brain, especially its pre-frontal cortex. However, we cannot equate or reduce consciousness to the brain, as we found in Chapter 6.

SELF-KNOWLEDGE

Again, a person can make much meaning for herself and others if she knows her true self. Western and Eastern philosophies both emphasize the importance of knowing about one's self. Lao Tsu, the mythical founder of the religion Taoism, wrote that, "**Knowing oneself is enlightenment.**" The Hindu scriptures tell how **self-knowledge alone brings bliss.** Socrates asserted in his defense of his philosophical way of life, "The Apology," that the main commandment of his philosophy is to "**know thyself.**"

Self-knowledge gives you an immediate or direct awareness of your sensations, thoughts, consciousness, attitudes and all mental states. Some philosophers such as Kant optimistically maintain that we can know all these just by reflecting on them. Most philosophers today, however, hold that we need some empirical observations, for example, one's sensations, to make the ideal theory of self-knowledge or, in other words, to know yourself fully. Yet, this reduces or lowers philosophy to psychology.

Although self-knowledge is directly available to each person, it paradoxically often turns out to be quite obscure and hard to obtain because it is so elusive.

Aristotle defined "the self" as "the essence of a person." He thought that the self did not exist apart from a body, but he did think that its intellect was immortal and in the perpetual motion of thinking. Aristotle emphasized that the self consists of its actual effects because this realizes its potentials. The main one for the human self is thinking. This is the essence of the self, for him. (A philosopher can choose no other. Ha! Ha yet still again!)

Aristotle maintained that the self has four parts: 1. the rational or calculating used for making decisions, 2. the vegetative, 3. the desiring and 4. the irrational. The last three parts identify one's needs. When one's body dies and decomposes, one's intellect or soul goes on thinking, according to him.

Many other philosophers likewise argue that thinking is the essence of the self. For example, while imprisoned in a castle, Islamic philosopher Avicenna wrote his "floating man" thought- experiment. He told his readers to imagine themselves "suspended in the air" isolated from all sensations, including those of their own bodies. He maintained that even in this scenario a person would still have self-consciousness. This led him to conclude that the self is independent of the body.

As American philosopher Wilfred Sellars expressed the matter recently, **the self should be regarded as a "given" or independently existing being.** Descartes even in the seventeenth century had written that he could imagine doubting all things and sensations, but not the sense of self itself. **Even to doubt this involves the self because doubting is a type of thinking. Pretty clever, huh?**

SKEPTICAL PHILOSOPHIES OF THE SELF

David Hume

Skeptical philosopher David Hume denied the view that we have a substantial self. He maintained that when we think about the self we never find anything but a bunch of sensations: "man [that is, a human] is nothing but a collection or bundle of different perceptions which follow each other with inconceivable rapidity." Hume did not think that that unifies the self into a soul. He compared the self to a commonwealth which keeps its identity by many different ways, mostly in the body. Hume enigmatically wrote in the "Appendix" to his massive Essay on Human Understanding that he was dissatisfied with his philosophy of the self, but he never wrote on this obtuse topic again. This does not much encourage us!

BUDDHA'S DENIAL OF THE SELF

Buddha

Hume's skeptical philosophy of the self is quite similar to those of the Buddha. This Asian philosopher held that the self consists only of what he called "transient aggregates" such as perceiving, sensing, emoting and willing. Traditional Buddhists today doubt that any grounds exist for an unchanging self or soul. They do not answer their skeptical questions as "Who is the bearer of the bundle?" and "What carries the aggregates?" Their answers to such questions are unequivocally, "Nothing permanent!"

Buddha attacked all attempts that defend a substantial self. **The Awakened One (what his name translates as) refused to define "the self" to deter us from "clinging" to the illusion that we have one.** We should instead think that the self is separated from all that truly is.

Buddha implored us to be "detached" from one's self and material things because these are not lasting. They can be enjoyed—Buddha is often shown in sculptures as gently smiling and with a fat belly—but they will not endure. **Only selfless union with all that exists will last,**

he maintained. This sounds quite inscrutable to westerners who tend to glorify the self.

We can best overcome skeptical doubts about the self through the philosophy of knowing of rationalism because it emphasizes internal sources of knowing. **Descartes overcame his total doubts about his self by his indubitable (or not doubtable) insight, "I think, therefore I am**." (See Chapter 5 on "Rationalism.") He made much meaning as the acknowledged father of modern philosophy by inspiring much novel thinking on the self in its other practitioners, especially Wilhelm Leibniz and Benedict Spinoza. **So, it appears that we do have selves. This opens the possibility that we may have immortal souls.** Let's examine this prospect now.

ARGUMENTS FOR THE SOUL

Souls have immortality defined as "the never-ending continuing of a person's self, even after the death of her body." **The endless amount of time involved in immortality makes it highly meaningful to know whether on not it exists for us.** Let us now explore the main arguments for the soul, then for its immortality.

The main argument for the existence of the soul is that human thinking differs too much in many ways from physical things, especially the brain. (See Chapter 6 on "Arguments for Intangibles," especially for consciousness.)

This main argument for the soul thereby implies that humans consist of two substances or natures: a physical body and a spiritual soul. **Since the soul is immaterial, it cannot die a material death. As it does not consist of physical parts, it cannot dissolve or fall apart.** The soul might well be identical with one's intangible mind, as

Descartes maintained, which can give us big truths. (See start of Chapter 5.)

(Some Asian philosophies and religions such as Hinduism and Buddhism maintain that the soul migrates from a dead body to re-incarnate in another one until it unites with the divinity from which it is separated. However, there is very little evidence of any kind for this view, just traditional beliefs.)

ARGUMENTS FOR THE IMMORTALITY OF THE SOUL

Plato presented four arguments for the immortality of the soul in his dialogue, "Phaedo," named after the student who relates them. This student presents these arguments as those of Socrates who shortly awaits being executed by drinking the terrifying poison hemlock, which was rumored then to freeze a person's body from the toes up to the heart. Yet, these arguments are clearly Plato's, as Socrates himself wrote nothing.

1. **Plato called his first argument the "cyclical" one. It is based on Plato's extremely complex philosophy of Ideas** (again, capitalized because he maintained that they are eternal, independent and unchanging realities, far different from the subjective thoughts that we conceive of them today).

   Since the soul always brings life to a body, it must be an Idea which has life or power according to Plato. (See "Intangibles Have Power" in Chapter 6.) Socrates called the soul "imperishable." He described it as the total opposite of the body. The living comes from the dead in a cycle. The dead are generated through death from the living, and vice versa. Yet, this argument is more circular than cyclical.

Socrates made an analogy (or comparison) of the soul to fire and cold, stating that if cold gets close to its opposite, fire, it must withdraw intact. The soul does this when the body dies.

Socrates also compared the soul to the poles of a magnet. Just as the same poles of a magnet repel each other, so does the life of the soul repel death. This is a basic law of physics that the soul must obey, Socrates argued.

2. **The argument from recollection is based on perfect, non- empirical knowledge that a person recalls from her soul's previous existence, for example, knowing about perfect equality**. A person must get this knowledge of perfection from her previous existence. So the soul existed before the birth of one's body. In Plato's dialogue Meno he boldly proclaimed that we are born with all our knowledge from previous lives. Which knowledge we realize depends on what we discover of it in various ways. He held from these considerations that the soul must be re-born.

This is not one of his strongest arguments because the only perfect knowledge that we have is strictly mental from relationships of ideas to each other.

3. **The argument from affinity (or similarity) maintains that the soul most resembles that which is invisible, divine and eternal rather than their opposites**. So when one's physical body dies, her soul continues because it is very different. It has an affinity for the immortal. We did find that the soul does differ much from the mortal body in Chapter 6 on intangibles.

4. **The argument from participating in the Ideas argues that the Idea of the soul participates in the eternal nature of the Idea of life in general, and so it can never die itself. The soul is the cause of life,**

according to Plato. To be alive, a body must participate in the Idea of a soul which is absolute. (Recall here that scientists have been unable to create life by combining chemicals.) Because the soul so participates it will endure being annihilated as, for example, will the number three. The soul cannot be converted to its opposite which is death. This difficult dialogue concludes that our souls will exist in another world. (I already have briefly commented in Chapter 6 on the strengths and weaknesses of Plato's arguing from the metaphor of participating.)

Plato's arguments for the immortality of the soul are extremely theoretical and abstract, indeed. It is quite hard to evaluate them because of this, especially since they stem from his enormously complex philosophy of Ideas which no one except him could comprehend. **Plato's arguments for the immortality of the soul thus disappoint everyone who reads them.**

Yet, it is clear that no one, except perhaps Christian martyrs contemplating the beatific vision of God, have embraced the death of his body more courageously than Socrates. He welcomed this as freeing his soul from the shackles of his body, unperturbed by the death of the body and inspired by an after-life full of goodness from thinking. This surely frees prisoners from the cave of the senses. (See Chapter 2.) Yet, he left this issue to each person to think about on her own by his final remark The Apology that only God knows about the immortality of the soul.

THE RESURRECTION OF THE BODY

The resurrection of the body is a physical form of the argument for the immortality of the self. This argument dispenses with the intangible of the soul. It maintains that **one's dead body will be restored to life as an imperishable glorified body, according to Paul of Tarsus,** who was the leading Christian advocate of resurrection.

Jesus said about it only that "if you destroy this temple [his body], I shall resurrect it." He apparently was struggling with his belief in resurrected bodies sometimes mentioned in Hebrew scriptures.

Jesus clearly resurrected according to the Gospels selected by the Catholic Church. His resurrected body was glorified, as he passed through a wall in the upper room to talk to his assembled apostles and disciples. The Gospels emphasize that he was fleshy after he resurrected. He stated that all humankind would resurrect at "the end of the present time" --whenever that is! --and "in the world to come,"--wherever that is!-- according to the Nicene Creed, which established early Catholic Church doctrines.

Note that the resurrection of the body makes no reference to the soul which is a Greek idea foreign to the entire Middle East where Christianity arose. Yet, perhaps because the immortal soul is so optimistic, it became a major part of Christian doctrine, especially after the Renaissance with its great love of Greek ideas. Christians found the doctrine of the immortal soul meaningful emotionally and optimistically. **They combined the soul with resurrection which has much meaning to them so that they can physically see and be with their loved ones in Heaven forever without dying.**

Doesn't it appear that Christians on the after-life of the self are believing what they want to believe rather than what they can know to be true by evidence which they ought to go by according to the laws of logic and knowing? (See Chapters 4 and 5.) It seems quite so, but **remember yet still again that such subjective views make little meaning, no matter how much a person deceives herself about them. She will not have much objective meaning.** Name someone who did. I myself cannot name anyone. (See Chapter 3 on how to make meaning.)

EXERCISES:

1. Why or why not do you think that you have a substantial self?

2. Do you consider any of the arguments for the immortality of the soul strong, especially Plato's four of them? Do you think that you have an immortal soul?

3. Do you think that your body will resurrect after it dies?

4. If you think that you will have a resurrected body, what glorified form do you think that it will take?

Chapter 11

MAKING MEANING BY POLITICAL PHILOSOPHY

Everyone today lives in a political society, that is, an urban one governed by laws. This fact alone makes political philosophy quite meaningful. **Every intelligent person ought to inquire into whether her society is just or unjust.** ("Just" is synonymous with "fair.") **This is the highest value in political philosophy. The justice of a society determines whether or not an individual can make much meaning in it.**

Political philosophy has many other questions than what is justice. Some of the main ones beside just laws include the following: fair enforcing of the laws, freedom or liberty, duties to the state, rights, the environment, race relations (especially in the U. S.), the equality of women and gay people and the just punishment of law-breakers?

Clearly, political philosophy is highly meaningful because it covers many areas of our daily lives in our societies.

This chapter will focus on justice as the main guiding idea of society in political philosophy. **A society cannot have too much justice, although it can have too much freedom and equality**, according to Mortimer Adler. **You can best make meaning in political philosophy by knowing what justice is.**

Fairly distributing justice, especially in its education and economics, is a society's biggest problem, especially for those born poor, as we shall shortly read. Some politicians are corrupt, but justice should not be because you cannot make much meaning in society without knowing what it is. Government controls much of society, especially the economy, thereby jobs.

It might seem hard to know what justice is, but all you need is a meaningful idea of it, for examples from some philosophers on it:

Jefferson thought justice was freedom of individuals;

Martin Luther King preached that it was Christian love of every-one, including even those whom you do not like and who treat you with prejudice;

and Abraham Lincoln felt strongly that it was the unity of people, especially in the North and South of the United States.

Plato observed how society is a collection of individuals. He further observes that they ought to be ethical so society does not destroy itself. (See Chapter 7 on "Why Be Ethical?") Since this is true, **applying ethics to society is a main task of political philosophy.** A very brief summary of ethics in Chapter 7 includes the following main applications of ethics to society:

Ethics

tells us what is the complex idea of the good;

teaches people how to live a good life;

tells you what you ought to do in every major moral decision;

sets high standards for us to live in accordance with;

teaches us to be pro-active in helping others;

tells a people how to be happy;

explains strong reasons for being ethical rather than not; and

gives us many moral absolutes to avoid widespread spineless relativism. (See Chapter 7 on ethics.)

If all the citizens of a society practiced these main points of ethics, there would clearly be no injustices and no need for political philosophy. **The first requirement of a just society is therefore that individuals in it be ethical.**

A major part of being just includes being equitable or treating all others as equal in respect of their dignity.

Statue of Justicia

Justice is symbolized in the allegorical statue of Justicia. She has a sword to symbolize her swift and final authority to enforce justice. The scales stand for measuring conflicting claims. Her blindfold represents her impartiality in dispensing justice without regard to wealth, class and the like. **Plato envisioned justice as the harmony or the proper balance of classes in their society under the guidance of a philosopher-king.** (See "Why Be Ethical?" in Chapter 7.) Yet, he doubted that justice is possible on Earth. He had witnessed the framed-up murder of Socrates who sought to know what is justice.

No society has yet balanced for long the claims of society with those of individuals, especially if they are born poor or a discriminated minority, according to Mortimer Adler. Education can bring about such a balance, but public schools in big cities typically are poor.

Plato thought that **a society would be just only if it has a philosopher as its king or leader because only, she has wisdom to apply Ideas to the practices of our daily lives in society.** (See Chapter 2 on "Plato on Wisdom.")

Throughout history, thinkers have developed justice on the basis of various philosophies. Some main examples of these are divine commands, natural laws, a tacit social contract (agreement) and useful consequences for the largest number of people.

However, **the best basis of justice is that individuals make meaning in their societies.** What could be more just than individuals making a positive impact in their societies? Obviously, nothing!

TYPES OF INJUSTICES

Karl Marx

Awareness of the types of injustices can clarify what is justice, a good society and making meaning in it. The following are some main types of injustices:

ECONOMIC INJUSTICE is the basic type, according to philosopher Karl Marx, because the amount of money that a person has determines the quality of her life. Most societies, including the U. S., have far too much poverty in which a person cannot live a good life. **Being poor often depends on the accidents of one's birth. A person has no control over this**. A just society provides for the financial welfare of all its citizens, as does Denmark for health care, for example. **It is quite difficult for a person to make much meaning, even for herself, without enough money.**

INJUSTICES IN THE WORKPLACE are common because most workers in the U. S. are "at will" unless they have a contract. They can be fired at any time for no reason. This is quite unjust because a worker devotes much of her life to work. Many jobs do not pay a living wage, whereas owners are typically wealthy. **Many jobs today**

also are so stressful that most workers have little energy to make meaning after they finish working. Most workers today have time at night largely only to play on their cell-phones and watch vapid videos or programs on television.

THE MILITARY BUDGET takes a huge part of our taxes ($681 billion in 2019), more than 60%. **The military's main purpose is strictly to kill enemies who are strangers, often in unjust wars.** (See Chapter 6 on "How We Live For Intangibles" on peace.) **This maximizes injustice.** It returns very little to the economy except to employ people as soldiers temporarily at very low wages.

RACISM has been present in the U. S. since it was largely taken most unfairly from the "Indians" out of sheer greed. It wrongly regards groups of people as having inheritable traits of behavior, for example, laziness. **Racists divide these groups on the basis of the supposed superiority of one race over another who are then treated with prejudice. Racism is scientifically false as well as unjust.** It has played a major role in genocides, particularly the atrocious Nazi Holocaust in Europe during World War II.

Today there is much racial segregating in schools and housing, especially in affluent American suburbs. The U. S. in effect has made two separate societies, one for the rich and one for the poor. This is highly unjust. **It is extremely hard for a person to make much meaning if she is a victim of racial prejudice from birth.**

SEXISM treats women as inferior to men. Feminists (or believers in the equality in dignity of women) maintain that **the sexes or genders ought to be equal in all basic regards.** Women today have far fewer positions of power and get paid lower wages than men in the same jobs. Preventing sexual assault and violence, especially rape, and harassment are major projects of feminists. **Raising a family as a**

mother while also having a demanding career much challenges most women now. In general, women have less access to opportunities than do men today. The ability to make meaning should not depend on one's gender which is irrelevant to justice.

I have presented many injustices so that the reader will not naively think that her country is totally just and that it is easy to make meaning in society, as she was probably indoctrinated.

Can you eliminate any of these injustices? That would make much meaning, but would be quite hard simply because of the huge size of society. You can at best try to lessen these injustices in your life, but even that would also be very difficult to do again because of the overwhelming size of society. Trying to change society in basic ways almost always proves to be highly frustrating.

So, you can make most meaning by political philosophy by striving to be just, especially in ethical ways, in your own life. Even that would be quite an achievement!

EXERCISES:

1. Drawing from the ideas discussed in this chapter, what do you think makes a just society?

2. Discuss what you think is the biggest injustice in the U. S. today. Why do you think that it is the biggest one? What can you do make it less of an injustice?

3. What can an individual do to make her society a more just place in which to live?

4. Summarize how you can best live a just life.

Chapter 12

ARE YOU FREE OR CAUSED?

"Free will" is defined as "a person's ability to choose from alternatives." If a person is free, she is morally responsible and praiseworthy or blameworthy for her actions. She might feel guilty or even sinful (if she is religious) about them. She also might feel horrible regret at her poor past choices, for example, one that led to her bad marriage. Should she forgive herself for this?

On the other hand, the argument from causes maintains that there are always concrete reasons or causes for every human action. This argument maintains that she should not blame herself for her poor past decisions or feel badly about them. These views on causes directly conflict with those of free will.

Whether free or caused, you can make meaning, but **you make much more meaning if you are free** because you have dignity.

Your philosophy on free will therefore is highly meaningful to your views on all other people because you regard them in the same ways as yourself on this basic question.

You can make much meaning if you know how to make free choices for yourself.

Your philosophy on free will affects all the following big beliefs about people, including yourself:

are you **responsible** for your actions;

are you **praiseworthy** or blameworthy;

are you a **guilty sinner** (if you are

spiritual);

should you **forgive** yourself;   and

perhaps most importantly, should **you be critical of a person or should we try to understand her behavior in terms of her causes?**

People have much dignity if they are free, but do they if they are caused? No, they all are just what they are made to be by their causes. How much respect do you owe a person in each case? You owe them much if they are free, but respect is not even relevant if they are caused because reasons make them do what they do.

As often in philosophy, very much meaning is here at stake. A person can make much meaning if she knows how she can free herself from her causes. I will discuss how to do so at the end of this chapter.

The free-will question is "can humans make free choices or are they always caused to do everything that they do?" The main argument against free will is, again, that all actions and choices are caused. A "cause" is defined as a concrete reason that makes anything, event and even choice happen. **Everything must have causes that make it happen in the exact way that it does. In effect, causes force things to happen, including human choices,** as I will explain shortly.

Free will cannot explain anything, especially one's choices. These would be totally arbitrary without having causes to explain them.

THE ARGUMENT FROM CAUSES THAT HUMANS DO NOT HAVE FREE WILL

Causes usually do not make things (effects) happen in obvious ways to us. They are often complex combinations of connected factors, for examples, all of a person's environment and her relationships to friends, fellow workers and especially her parent's loving or abusive treatment of her. As an adult she acts these causes out. **Effects often happen over a prolonged period of time,** although some of them happen immediately.

Without the notion of causes there would be no natural or social sciences. **The fundamental law of science is that there must be a cause for everything that happens to explain it. This law clearly applies to humans.** The sciences are our most reliable way of knowing factual truths—not the big truths of philosophy—and have much transformed the world when they were applied to it, especially in the form of technology.

Let's continue to explore the free-will question by first examining more of the argument that humans are caused (and hence not free) by considering the main factors in causes.

Again, the argument from causes holds that all our behavior results from many causes or forces over which we have no control.

This argument challenges you to name one example of an action that was not caused. This example would be quite hard to give! None of my students in forty years of my teaching in five states could give such an example.

The causal argument maintains that we can predict all behavior if we know all the causes involved in it. Such knowledge would be quite hard to get because it would be quite detailed, but it can be gotten.

SOME MAIN KINDS OF CAUSES:

1. **THE ENVIRONMENT consists of all the conditions in which a person lives from her birth.** It is everything around her that has any influence on her or that she experiences. The main factor at first is her parents. They determine the social and economic class into which she is born which is highly influential. She has no control over this or even their treatment of her, even if this is abusive.

We can call this kind of causes a person's "conditioning" in addition to her "environment."

Many other main parts of a person's environment are influential in causing her behavior: extended family, friends, schools, churches and workplaces are just some of the main conditions. There are many, many other causal conditions of a person's behavior in her environment. A person experiences many environmental causes very early in her life. This makes them even more powerful because what you learn earliest in your life you learn best.

The combination of all these environmental causes is extremely powerful in determining a person's actions. It would be exceedingly hard to do otherwise than what they strongly influence a person to do, particularly in view of the other types of causes that accompany them. Again, only one action or choice can result from all of a person's causes in her environment.

Again, the effects of causes due to conditioning are rarely direct or immediate. They are cumulative, but quite powerful. One's causes by her conditioning certainly should not be dismissed or ignored when asking the free-will question. Look at how powerful the media and politicians are around the world in demanding that everyone wear masks and socially distance themselves when these are based on faulty science that did not slow the spread of the COVID-19 pandemic.

2. **THE SUBCONSCIOUS is another powerful kind of cause. It is the part of your mind that is beneath or beyond your conscious mind. As it consists of 90% of the brain's activity, it is a very strong cause.** The subconscious controls such bodily functions as breathing and heartbeat.

Dreams, repressed feelings and deep fears are examples of subconscious states and causes. Their purposes are to store data to ensure that you respond exactly as you were programmed to fit a pattern consistent with your self-concept.

The subconscious is often a theme of ancient Greek drama, especially Sophocles' "Oedipus Rex." Oedipus unknowingly kills his father and marries his mother. (Freud argued that this verifies his views on sex.) Indicating his subconscious causes, Paul of Tarsus wrote, "That which I would not do, I do." He realized well that his conscious will is like a slave to his subconscious motives that caused his actions despite his strong conscious beliefs.

3. **GENETIC INHERITANCE causes a person to be the kind of person who she is because she inherits from her parents at the moment of conception certain traits that make her personality.** For example, a person who inherits genes that cause her to be highly intelligent will make choices that fit that personality, given that she has the proper causes in her environment to do so. This is cause and effect, albeit complex. However, most genetic inheritance is more complex than this. Genetic scientists now have growing evidence that traits are inherited from several generations in humans (and other highly evolved mammals). These scientists also now have discovered that there are 2,600 genes in each of our cells. No wonder that they are such strong causes of our behavior and choices!

How could you choose to do other than who you are caused to be as a person by your inherited genes along with the other types of causes?

According to the argument from causes, a person can make changes in her life, but only if she was fortunate or lucky enough to be born with such genes to make changes in her life.

Some reformers such as counselors and psychologists can cause others, particularly a criminal who suffered severe abuse in her childhood in a poverty-stricken neighborhood, which are environmental causes), to have good causes to rehabilitate themselves, but this would be extremely hard. **Reformers of people need to**

provide causes that are more powerful than all the criminal's previous powerful ones.

Did criminals freely commit their crimes? No, they were caused to do so by the factors mentioned in the above paragraphs. Otherwise, why would they subject themselves to such social ostracism and severe punishments, for example, confinement in prison?

The above are the main kinds of causes (conditioning, subconscious and genetic), but there are many others. When these are combined, a person cannot help but do what she is caused to do by many kinds of causes, claims the argument from causes. Is it correct? It is quite strong according to the laws of logic, but let's now examine the opposing arguments for free will.

THE MAIN ARGUMENTS FOR FREE WILL: DELIBERATION & LOVE

To make a free choice, a person must overcome all her powerful causes. This is certainly not easy! Can it even be done? The strongest argument that favors it in the history of philosophy, going back to Aristotle, who did not fully develop it, is from thinking hard or deliberating about one's causes. **Think hard to become more aware of your past causes. This can help you overcome them.**

The next step in making a free choice involves deep thinking of a choice that one was not caused to think. This step requires the thinker to engage in concentrated thinking to mentally explore other possibilities for her acting and thinking. If a new idea "pops" into her head, she will have freed herself from her causes. To do so, she needs to engage in some creative thinking to make a new idea, to her, come into existence. This creative thinking is quite advanced, the highest for humans. (See Chapter 4 on "Think Creatively.") However, anyone who has solved a practical problem has used creative thinking to overcome the blockage that caused it.

Such thinking is by no means easy, but it can be done on a regular basis. **If a person often thinks deliberately, that is deeply and creatively, she can even live a free life-style.**

EXAMPLES OF FREE WILL

Studying several examples of free choices can tell us how we can make them, and hence much meaning, for ourselves.

A student who studies philosophy or any subject primarily to learn about it exemplifies free will. She also might find its subject matter to be what students commonly call "interesting." On the other hand, if she studies any subject simply to get a good grade to increase her chances of getting her preferred job, she is clearly caused by this reason and so she is not free.

A more complicated example of free will comes from curing alcoholism. Some alcoholics have genetic causes of this disease such as severe genetic anxiety, whereas for others it is caused by highly adverse environmental conditions, particularly getting a low sense of self-esteem in her youth. **To be cured, an alcoholic must deliberate deeply to overcome these causes. She needs to think hard about other ways of living that make more meaning than being an alcoholic. She also needs to have new idea "pop" into her mind to start her thinking about how she can make more meaning than**

excessively drinking alcohol to escape from the gruesome reality of her past causes. In other words, she needs to think of how she can live a new lifestyle that is more meaningful than the alcoholic one. That is quite obviously hard to do, but it is what an alcoholic need to do to freely cure her disease.

The last example of a free choice suggests **a way in which a person can be free by finding something that she loves to free herself from all her causes. This is implied in Stanley Kubrick's surrealistic movie, "A Clockwork Orange."** In it the main character Alex is about to be killed by a woman's husband for raping her. Then he hears Beethoven's "Symphony #9" playing in the background. He much loves how this music symbolizes freedom. (See Chapter 8 on "Beethoven, Symphony #9.) Alex then freely jumps out of a window. He does not die, but he overcomes all his conditioning to his empty conformist society and abusive parents. He will now choose to do what he enjoys. At the end of the movie, Alex exclaims to himself in his hospital bed, "I am cured all right!"

Alex's enormous love of Beethoven's "Ninth Symphony" finally freed him from his horrible causes. If you can likewise find something that you love strongly, you can similarly free yourself from all your causes. Then you would be **"free at last!"** as Martin Luther King proclaimed about political freedom.

French Existentialist philosopher Sartre maintained that a person can always be free if she negates all her causes. To be free, he advises you to just say "No!" to your causes. We can be arbitrary and choose actions for no reason, for example, to go to a restaurant. Sartre implies that a person is free whenever she takes a chance.

You now know how to be free by deliberating and by strong love to choose to make meaning rather than being caused to do so. Start to do this now! Why not? Little can be greater in your life than to free yourself to make meaning!

EXERCISES:

1. Which two human actions do you think are likely to be free? Why?

2. Which two human actions do you think are caused? Why?

3. Explain one type of cause of human behavior that was not treated in this chapter.

4. Discuss one example of an action that is free by deliberating a new idea and one that is free by loving something.

5. Write one creative idea that you thought of that freed you to make your own choice.

6. Write something that you love that has freed you at least once.

Index